Joyce Appleby on *Thomas Jefferson*
Louis Auchincloss on *Theodore Roosevelt*
Jean H. Baker on *James Buchanan*
H. W. Brands on *Woodrow Wilson*
Douglas Brinkley on *Gerald R. Ford*
Josiah Bunting III on *Ulysses S. Grant*
James MacGregor Burns and Susan Dunn on *George Washington*
Charles W. Calhoun on *Benjamin Harrison*
Gail Collins on *William Henry Harrison*
Robert Dallek on *Harry S. Truman*
John W. Dean on *Warren G. Harding*
John Patrick Diggins on *John Adams*
E. L. Doctorow on *Abraham Lincoln*
Elizabeth Drew on *Richard M. Nixon*
Annette Gordon-Reed on *Andrew Johnson*
Henry F. Graff on *Grover Cleveland*
David Greenberg on *Calvin Coolidge*
Gary Hart on *James Monroe*
Hendrik Hertzberg on *Jimmy Carter*
Roy Jenkins on *Franklin Delano Roosevelt*
Zachary Karabell on *Chester Alan Arthur*
Lewis H. Lapham on *William Howard Taft*
William E. Leuchtenburg on *Herbert Hoover*
Timothy Naftali on *George Bush*
Kevin Phillips on *William McKinley*
Robert V. Remini on *John Quincy Adams*
Ira Rutkow on *James A. Garfield*
John Seigenthaler on *James K. Polk*
Hans L. Trefousse on *Rutherford B. Hayes*
Tom Wicker on *Dwight D. Eisenhower*
Ted Widmer on *Martin Van Buren*
Sean Wilentz on *Andrew Jackson*
Garry Wills on *James Madison*

Saint Augustine's Childhood: Confessions, Book I (translation)
Venice: Lion City
Papal Sin
A Necessary Evil: A History of American Distrust in Government
Saint Augustine
John Wayne's America
Certain Trumpets: The Call of Leaders
Witches and Jesuits: Shakespeare's Macbeth
Lincoln at Gettysburg: The Words That Remade America
Under God: Religion and American Politics
Nixon Agonistes
The Kennedy Imprisonment
Inventing America
Cincinnatus: George Washington and the Enlightenment
Explaining America
Lead Time
Chesterton
Politics and Catholic Freedom
Roman Culture
Jack Ruby
The Second Civil War
Bare Ruined Choirs
Confessions of a Conservative
At Button's

James
Madison

Garry Wills

James
Madison

THE AMERICAN PRESIDENTS SERIES

ARTHUR M. SCHLESINGER, JR., GENERAL EDITOR

Times Books

HENRY HOLT AND COMPANY, NEW YORK

Times Books
Henry Holt and Company, LLC
Publishers since 1866
175 Fifth Avenue
New York, New York 10010

Henry Holt® is a registered trademark of Henry Holt and Company, LLC.

Frontispiece: Engraving of James Madison © Bettmann/CORBIS

ISBN-13: 978-0-8050- 6905-1

Henry Holt books are available for special promotions and premiums.
For details contact: Director, Special Markets.

Printed in the United States of America

TO JOHN
my favorite historian

Contents

Editor's Note

THE AMERICAN PRESIDENCY

The president is the central player in the American political order. That would seem to contradict the intentions of the Founding Fathers. Remembering the horrid example of the British monarchy, they invented a separation of powers in order, as Justice Brandeis later put it, "to preclude the exercise of arbitrary power." Accordingly, they divided the government into three allegedly equal and coordinate branches—the executive, the legislative, and the judiciary.

But a system based on the tripartite separation of powers has an inherent tendency toward inertia and stalemate. One of the three branches must take the initiative if the system is to move. The executive branch alone is structurally capable of taking that initiative. The Founders must have sensed this when they accepted Alexander Hamilton's proposition in the Seventieth Federalist that "energy in the executive is a leading character in the definition of good government." They thus envisaged a strong president—but within an equally strong system of constitutional accountability. (The term *imperial presidency* arose in the 1970s to describe the situation when the balance between power and accountability is upset in favor of the executive.)

The American system of self-government thus comes to focus in the presidency—"the vital place of action in the system," as

Woodrow Wilson put it. Henry Adams, himself the great-grandson and grandson of presidents as well as the most brilliant of American historians, said that the American president "resembles the commander of a ship at sea. He must have a helm to grasp, a course to steer, a port to seek." The men in the White House (thus far only men, alas) in steering their chosen courses have shaped our destiny as a nation.

Biography offers an easy education in American history, rendering the past more human, more vivid, more intimate, more accessible, more connected to ourselves. Biography reminds us that presidents are not supermen. They are human beings too, worrying about decisions, attending to wives and children, juggling balls in the air, and putting on their pants one leg at a time. Indeed, as Emerson contended, "There is properly no history; only biography."

Presidents serve us as inspirations, and they also serve us as warnings. They provide bad examples as well as good. The nation, the Supreme Court has said, has "no right to expect that it will always have wise and humane rulers, sincerely attached to the principles of the Constitution. Wicked men, ambitious of power, with hatred of liberty and contempt of law, may fill the place once occupied by Washington and Lincoln."

The men in the White House express the ideals and the values, the frailties and the flaws, of the voters who send them there. It is altogether natural that we should want to know more about the virtues and the vices of the fellows we have elected to govern us. As we know more about them, we will know more about ourselves. The French political philosopher Joseph de Maistre said, "Every nation has the government it deserves."

At the start of the twenty-first century, forty-two men have made it to the Oval Office. (George W. Bush is counted our forty-third president, because Grover Cleveland, who served nonconsecutive terms, is counted twice.) Of the parade of presidents, a dozen or so lead the polls periodically conducted by historians and political scientists. What makes a great president?

Great presidents possess, or are possessed by, a vision of an ideal America. Their passion, as they grasp the helm, is to set the ship of state on the right course toward the port they seek. Great presidents also have a deep psychic connection with the needs, anxieties, dreams of people. "I do not believe," said Wilson, "that any man can lead who does not act . . . under the impulse of a profound sympathy with those whom he leads—a sympathy which is insight—an insight which is of the heart rather than of the intellect."

"All of our great presidents," said Franklin D. Roosevelt, "were leaders of thought at a time when certain ideas in the life of the nation had to be clarified." So Washington incarnated the idea of federal union, Jefferson and Jackson the idea of democracy, Lincoln union and freedom, Cleveland rugged honesty. Theodore Roosevelt and Wilson, said FDR, were both "moral leaders, each in his own way and his own time, who used the presidency as a pulpit."

To succeed, presidents not only must have a port to seek but they must convince Congress and the electorate that it is a port worth seeking. Politics in a democracy is ultimately an educational process, an adventure in persuasion and consent. Every president stands in Theodore Roosevelt's bully pulpit.

The greatest presidents in the scholars' rankings, Washington, Lincoln, and Franklin Roosevelt, were leaders who confronted and overcame the republic's greatest crises. Crisis widens presidential opportunities for bold and imaginative action. But it does not guarantee presidential greatness. The crisis of secession did not spur Buchanan or the crisis of depression spur Hoover to creative leadership. Their inadequacies in the face of crisis allowed Lincoln and the second Roosevelt to show the difference individuals make to history. Still, even in the absence of first-order crisis, forceful and persuasive presidents—Jefferson, Jackson, James K. Polk, Theodore Roosevelt, Harry Truman, John F. Kennedy, Ronald Reagan, George W. Bush—are able to impose their own priorities on the country.

The diverse drama of the presidency offers a fascinating set of tales. Biographies of American presidents constitute a chronicle of wisdom and folly, nobility and pettiness, courage and cunning, forthrightness and deceit, quarrel and consensus. The turmoil perennially swirling around the White House illuminates the heart of the American democracy.

It is the aim of the American Presidents series to present the grand panorama of our chief executives in volumes compact enough for the busy reader, lucid enough for the student, authoritative enough for the scholar. Each volume offers a distillation of character and career. I hope that these lives will give readers some understanding of the pitfalls and potentialities of the presidency and also of the responsibilities of citizenship. Truman's famous sign—"The buck stops here"—tells only half the story. Citizens cannot escape the ultimate responsibility. It is in the voting booth, not on the presidential desk, that the buck finally stops.

—Arthur M. Schlesinger, Jr.

Key to Brief Citations

Where numbers alone are cited (for example, 3.25), they refer to volume and page in *The Papers of James Madison*, edited by William T. Hutchinson et al. (University of Chicago Press, 1962–). Given the vagaries of eighteenth and early-nineteenth-century orthography (especially as reported in newspapers and official journals), I punctuate and spell all texts by modern standards, without changing a single word.

A   Henry Adams, *History of the United States of America During the Administrations of James Madison* (Library of America, 1986)

B   Irving Brant, *James Madison*, volumes 1–6 (Bobbs-Merrill Company, 1941–1961)

G   Henry Adams, *The Life of Albert Gallatin* (J. B. Lippincott & Co., 1879)

J   Julian Boyd et al., eds., *The Papers of Thomas Jefferson* (Princeton University Press, 1950–)

K   Ralph Ketcham, *James Madison* (University Press of Virginia, 1990)

P   Robert Allen Rutland et al., eds., *The Papers of James Madison, Presidential Series* (University Press of Virginia, 1984–)

R   Robert Allen Rutland, *The Presidency of James Madison* (University Press of Kansas, 1990)

RL   James Morton Smith, ed., *The Republic of Letters: The Correspondence Between Thomas Jefferson and James Madison, 1776–1826* (Norton, 1995)

S   J. C. A. Stagg, *Mr. Madison's War* (Princeton University Press, 1983)

James
Madison

Introduction:
The Problem

The year 1812 was a glorious one for Russia and Canada. Each repelled a would-be conqueror, Napoleon Bonaparte in Russia's case, James Madison in Canada's. Further humiliation was in store for both rulers in 1814, when they were extruded from their own capital cities, Napoleon exiled to Elba, Madison in flight from his incinerated residence. Admiral George Cockburn of the Royal Navy—the man who torched the White House after drinking a toast ("Jemmy's health!") in the president's captured wine—would later take the captive Napoleon to Saint Helena. We are all familiar with Madison on his way to Philadelphia, to craft the Constitution in 1787. We rarely think of the commander in chief of defeated armies returning to a pillaged Washington twenty-seven years later. No wonder "Mister Madison's War," as the Federalists called it in New England, has been described as "the forgotten war."

Madison's very presidency is semi-forgotten. When Madison expert Jack N. Rakove published a selection of his writings in 1999, only 40 of its 864 pages came from the presidential years. Earlier collections of Madison's writings scanted the same years. One— Gilpin's *Papers of James Madison* (1840)—omitted them altogether. And in Rakove's brief (180 pages) biography of Madison for the Library of American Biography series (1990), 35 pages are devoted to the two years in which Madison shepherded the Constitution to ratification, while only 24 pages are devoted to his eight years as president. The disproportion reflects a consensus that Madison, though one of the nation's greatest founders, is not one of its greatest presidents. The periodic ratings drawn up by historians reflect the same consensus. He is usually ranked among the "high-average" presidents, not among the top-ten "great" or "near great" ones.[1]

How a man could be so shining in certain aspects of his life and so shadowed in another is not a question often asked. It is the problem I would like this book to address—how to put together the shrewd constitutionalist and the hapless commander in chief. The normal approach has been to pay attention to the bright spots and just ignore the dimmer moments. Few have attempted to see any common traits in the man who planned the government brilliantly but was lackluster in conducting it. Explanation, I suppose, could take one of three approaches, based on circumstances, on temperament, or on specific errors.

1. *Circumstances.* One could say that Madison was just dealt a bad hand. It was a difficult time to be president, when an unwelcome war was almost forced upon him. There are several problems with this explanation. As we shall see, Madison actually welcomed the war. He schemed to bring it on. Besides, difficult times have summoned greatness from other men. A nation calls for leadership in the dire case— our greatest presidents have faced crises, including conflicts like the Civil War and the world wars. Other wars, admittedly, have left a cloudier legacy, mainly because they were less clear in rationale or outcome—Polk's Mexican war, McKinley's Spanish war, Truman's Korean war, or Nixon's Vietnam war. Does Mr. Madison's war belong with those more dubious conflicts? Not quite. For one thing, those other four were fought against weaker opponents (one of the things that made them less than stirring), whereas Madison took on the British Empire at the great moment when it rallied Europe to crush Napoleon. Two of the four other wars added territory to the country, but Madison failed in his attempt to add Canada to the United States. The other two of the four were fought against surrogates for another power we were trying to injure (Communist China). Madison's war was unlike any other in that it seemed to gain nothing, yet it added to his popularity.

We can hardly say that circumstances defeated the man who left office more admired than he had been when he entered it eight years earlier. He completed two terms and passed on the office to a chosen successor within his party and within his administration, his own secretary of state, James Monroe. After all, in the twentieth century, only five of seventeen presidents have succeeded in completing two full terms, and only two of those passed on the office to a successor of his own party. Perhaps circumstances were more adverse in the twentieth than in the nineteenth century.

2. *Temperament.* This is a sounder explanation. Madison's major achievements reflect a legislative talent. He worked best in conventions or congresses. He was our best committeeman. But he had no real executive experience before he became president. He was not, like his three predecessors, a successful governor, ambassador, or leader of armies. He had been a colonel of militia, but only as a twenty-four-year-old subaltern to his father in Orange County. He was not a charismatic figure. His voice and his nerves were weak—he thought himself epileptic. He was small enough (five feet four inches and one hundred pounds) to be called "withered" by Washington Irving (B 5.239), "mean" (meager) by the British minister in America (K 496), and "a pigmy" by a Federalist critic (K 597).[2] He did not like to put himself forward—he let his larger and louder wife act as his surrogate in many personal relationships.

He worked best not merely in committee but in secret. Things that are now among his best-known achievements were done covertly, anonymously, or pseudonymously at the time—his arguments at the Constitutional Convention (whose record he kept secret all his life), his contributions to *The Federalist*, his composition of the best defense of religious freedom *(Memorial and Remonstrance)*, his authorship of the Virginia Resolutions and the *Report* defending them, his pseudonymous pamphleteering for Jefferson and ghostwriting for Washington. In the latter role he performed the feat, during his own first term in the House of Representatives, of writing Washington's inaugural address, writing the House's response to it, writing Washington's thank-you for that response, as well as Washington's thanks to the Senate's response. As the editors of his papers say, in this entire transaction "Madison was in dialogue with himself" (12.120).

He was often a semi-silent collaborator with more dramatic men—with Hamilton in calling the Constitutional Convention and composing *The Federalist;* with Washington in conduct of the

Constitutional Convention and planning the federal city; with Jefferson as his secretary of state and fellow regent of the University of Virginia. In the Mutt-and-Jeff collaboration with giants like Washington and Jefferson, it would be easy to overlook (literally) the man who was about a foot shorter than the more public actor. Madison, in fact, so often played the role of junior partner that critics felt he could not be president all on his own but was still responding, in the White House, to strings held by Jefferson at Monticello.

It is true, then, that by temperament and talent he was better equipped to be a legislator than an executive. Is that all we need to know for explaining his shortcomings as a president? Was his record strong before he entered the White House because it involved legislative duties merely? And did it turn instantly bad as soon as he was ensconced in office because whole new duties, executive ones, now devolved on him for the first time? I think there is more to it than that.

3. *Errors.* Madison brought to the presidency two equal-but-opposite errors, two misreadings of the British Empire—as frighteningly powerful inside the boundaries of the United States, and as surprisingly weak outside those borders. These should have been mutually canceling conceptions, but the peculiarity of Madison's outlook and history made them mutually reinforcing. In conjunction, they had misled him before he came to the presidency—they were behind Madison's obsession with Hamilton, which caused the great swerve in his thinking during the 1790s. They supplied the basis for the ill-conceived embargo that Jefferson imposed at his prompting. They are what made him welcome the prospect of war with England, and bring it on just when all other rationales for it were evanescing.

So it is not true to think of the pre-presidential and presidential years as separate entities, with a bright line drawn between them by his election as chief executive. Common traits run through both periods, and are based on two neglected qualities in Madison's makeup. These are not emphasized in most treatments of Madison because they do not need to be. Historians not trying to make sense of his presidency can explain his earlier achievements in terms of undoubted strengths, which were of a very high order. But he did have his weak points. These show up early in his political life, but they are not much adverted to because they did not have the large-scale effects that they would have when he was president. These weak points were a certain provincialism with regard to the rest of the world and a certain naivete with regard to the rest of his fellow human beings. The provincialism was spotted by Hamilton, who told Britain's minister that Madison was "very little acquainted with the world."[3] The naivete was noticed by George Clinton, who was Madison's as well as Jefferson's vice president, and who said that Madison had "too little practical knowledge" (S 53).

The provincialism would have been disturbed if he had been exposed to England in any direct way. Unfortunately, he was one of four early secretaries of state who had never been outside the boundaries of his own nation. (Such nominations could not be made now, since the Senate would not confirm them.) The other three—Edmund Randolph under Washington, Timothy Pickering under Adams, and Robert Smith in his own administration—did not perform well.[4] Though Madison was more intelligent and loyal than they were, he foisted on Jefferson his worst policy, the embargo, which was enough to make Jefferson's second term end in near disgrace. And the embargo was a product of Madison's provincialism. England had to be taken on, because it was still influential with America's own "anglomen." It could be taken on safely, because it was so vulnerable to American trade pressures. Madison's mental map was a little like the map on a famous *New Yorker* cover, where the American continent dwindles rapidly off from an outsize New York. On Madison's map it was Europe that shrank in proportion to its distance from our shores.

The naivete that George Clinton noticed came from Madison's bookish remove from others. He was what the eighteenth century called a man of the cabinet, not of the field. He was a prodigious worker at his desk, an omnivorous reader. But his social relations were such that he did not even try to woo a woman until he was thirty-one, and then he chose an apparently easy target—the fifteen-year-old daughter of a man who admired him. She responded to his courting, apparently to please her father, but soon found a younger man more to her liking. Madison was so humiliated by this rejection that he later scored out the passage in a coded letter to Jefferson in which he told him of his suit (6.481). That was understandable. What is less admirable is that he wrote in the margin that the code of the passage was "undecipherable." He blackened it precisely because it was decipherable. We shall find him rewriting retrieved letters from Jefferson on matters more political. In fact, Madison showed a marked penchant for doctoring the records of his life. The man of the cabinet shrank from some of the ways the outside world failed to correspond with his neat schematizations of it.

He did not approach a woman again for another twelve years, when he asked for the hand of a merry widow, Dolley Payne Todd, who was seventeen years his junior. He asked Aaron Burr to serve as his go-between and spokesman (Burr had roomed in the boarding-house run by Mrs. Todd's mother). After a quick courtship, Madison delegated many of the social functions that made him uncomfortable to the effusive Dolley, who performed them brilliantly for her "great little Madison."[5] They were an odd but loving couple—he quiet in the corner at her salon, dressed in conservative black, his thin pow-dered hair combed forward to cover (ineffectually) his baldness; she circulating everywhere, setting female fashions for wearing turbans of imported fabric, keeping necklines low, and taking snuff.

Some of his retired bearing came from bad health, which had made him expect a short life after early attacks of what he consid-ered epileptic breakdowns. When he was twenty-one, he told his Princeton friend that he could not make plans for the future since "my sensations of many months past have intimated to me not to expect a long or healthy life" (1.75). When asked later to travel abroad on political assignments, he said that his nerves were not up to it—he wrote Jefferson in 1785 that "crossing the sea would be unfriendly to a singular disease of my constitution" (8.270). These were not the only times when concern for his health confirmed his provincialism. Even as president he spent as much time on his own plantation as he could, trying not to return to Washington even in times of crisis, when his secretary of the Treasury, Albert Gallatin, said that he was desperately needed. He preferred to receive reports on what was happening at second hand. (Think, for con-trast, of Abraham Lincoln haunting the telegraph office adjacent to the White House.) Madison wanted a filter, to let him consider things at some remove from immediate pressures. He thought remoteness an advantage, as in his theory of representatives in an extended republic. In most legislative contexts, he was probably right. But the United States presidency is not a legislative office. No wonder Leonard White thought he would have been happier as president of the University of Virginia than as president of the country (P 1.xxi). Madison, picking his way through life with a careful monitoring of his own reactions, distanced himself from the way other people react to the immediacy of events.

"Impractical" in Clinton's word, he became naive about the chances his favored schemes had in the real world. What was self-evident in the cabinet, he felt, should be accepted without question in the field. Over and over he refused to give up on proposals whose intellectual elegance had delighted him as he drew them up. In the Continental Congress, he wanted a navy that would compel the states to pay their quotas for defense—he saw it as a domino effect, the coastal cities reacting to naval pressure, and the inland cities reacting to coastal cities. At the Constitutional Convention, he wanted a national veto on state laws. In drawing up the Bill of Rights, he wanted to enforce the same rights in the states as he was defining at the federal level. A man more worldly wise would have seen that none of these ideas had the slightest chance of being accepted at the time. All of them were quickly rejected, despite his repeated efforts to revive them; so they have not left an impression of this impractical side to Madison's character. The embargo was his one dreamy notion that was put into practice, and he never did see how mistaken that was. He kept wanting to reimpose it while he was president.

In order to trace the strands of continuity between the more familiar Madison of his early years and his less studied presidential time, I preface the main section of this book with a quick survey of his life up to his election as chief executive, to bring out some of the elements in his character that come to many as a surprise but were there all along. This will, I hope, show that Madison's shortcomings as president were not entirely a freak of circumstance or an accident of temperament. The weakness of his presidency was not solely, though it was partly, a product of the nation's situation in 1809, when he took office. My first three chapters are not, therefore, a balanced account of his life. They look through a filter that singles out elements to help explain what went wrong—and, for that matter, what went right—in his presidency. The final assessment of his performance in office must balance virtues with faults. I lay initial stress on the faults because the question most people have about his presidency is this: Why did it fall below the level of excellence reached in other areas of his life? That is the problem.

I.

Pre-presidential Years

(1751–1809)

1

———

Before the Constitution
(1751–1785)

We are all creatures of our time and place. But Madison's time and place enmeshed him in especially dense networks of both restraint and support, networks from which he never broke free, since he never wished to be free of them. Though he became very cosmopolitan in his reading and study, there was always a residue of provincialism in him. It came from his desire to remain in the cocoon of Virginia connections woven all about him. His wife, when he retired from the presidency, wanted him to see Paris with her. He went back to his father's home and stayed there the rest of his life, venturing out only once from his own neighborhood, and then only after twelve years had passed, and then only to another Virginia place: Richmond.

The Madison family had held plantations in various sections of its native state for a century before James's birth in 1751. The currency of influence was the land one held. Social functions were measured in relation to it. Lawyers served by vindicating land titles, politicians by protecting land interests, the professions by providing services to the plantations, the arts by refining their "great houses" as seats of authority. There were no major cities because the nodes of social and economic activity were those great houses. Getting some land counted for little, since there was so much of it. Large amounts of it gave one entry into the informal club that controlled the state's workings. Keeping and expanding one's holdings meant intermarrying within the club. The Madisons had married "up"—into the Taylor, Conway, and Catlett families. The brother of Madison's Taylor grandmother was the father of President Zachary Taylor.

The clergyman who presided over Madison's baptismal font was a relative, and so were the three godmothers and three godfathers clustered around the baby. Madison never moved out of this network of landholding "connections." His wife would later say that they streamed into his plantation by the hundreds. Madison's relatives, at this or that remove, included his namesake, Bishop James Madison, the president of the College of William and Mary (one of Jefferson's scientific collaborators); the legal giant (and Madison's political sponsor) Edmund Pendleton; the agrarian theorist (and Madison's schoolmate) John Taylor of Caroline. The in-law "cousins" included Andrew Lewis, one of Washington's in-laws, and Patrick Henry, his least favorite connection, who was related by marriage to his wife Dolley as well as to himself (K 4–7).

Being embedded in this weave of relationships gave a person a kind of social safety net. Madison grew up in a realm ruled by his namesake-father, who would live until James Junior—called Jemmy to distinguish him from James Senior—was fifty. All that time Madison lived in his father's house, supported even in his adulthood by a father who appreciated his genius. James Senior was the principal slave holder of Orange County—which made him, almost ex officio, justice of the peace, vestryman of the church, and commander of the county militia. These external duties were superadded to his responsibilities for the hundreds of acres and his "family" of 150 or so persons—free, slave, and kindred "subjects" over whom he had authority. A plantation owner had to perform many functions—as fiscal officer, agronomist, director of the commissary (so many shoes and shirts to keep supplying), adjudicator of disputes, dispenser of punishments, and minister of health. In the latter role, Madison's father had to make sure a midwife was always on hand for the many slave births (K 11), and the son was obliged, in his father's absence, to monitor an operation on a slave's tumor (1.190).

The whole system depended on authority and discipline. The master unable to manage this complex operation was soon debilitated by debt, shamed by relatives he let down, or driven to drink.

Madison admired the way his father performed his duties. As the eldest of ten children, Jemmy had to set an example, tend his siblings, and uphold his father's authority before relatives and slaves, responsibilities he assumed with entire loyalty. In 1775, as the Revolution began, the twenty-four-year-old Madison became colonel of the Orange County militia, serving as his father's highest-ranking subaltern, drilling and participating in rifle practice (1.153, 163–64). Though it is hard for us to imagine a less convincing soldier than this short frail man, it was just as hard for his neighbors to imagine him *not* playing that role. He was born to it. In fact, his militia service did not last long, since he was elected in 1776 (age twenty-five) to the colony's revolutionary convention in Williamsburg. He was not re-elected the next year, since the twenty-six-year-old aristocrat disdained the election practice of providing drinks and jollity at the polls. It was the only election he would ever lose. And even then his connections came to his rescue—he was appointed to Governor Patrick Henry's Council.

Madison's revolutionary zeal went along with the authority of his father in these early days of the Revolution. James and his peers insisted on a loyalty oath in Orange County, "that being [said the younger James] the method used among us to distinguish friends from foes and to oblige the common people to a more strict observance" (1.135). This reference to the common people reflects the glee with which Madison boasted to his college friend in Philadelphia, William Bradford, that "a fellow was lately tarred and feathered for treating one of our county committees with disrespect" (1.141). Respect was a big part of Madison's world, even when it had to be violently compelled. He approved of a threat to a parson who had not observed the fast called for by the Committee on Safety: "I question, should his insolence not abate, if he does not get decked in a coat of tar and surplice of feathers" (1.161). That kind of menace, he was glad to say, had made another non-observer "very supple and obsequious" (1.161). At the Virginia Convention of 1776, he voted for a harsh anti-Tory law (five years in prison for disloyal speech), and when he was back in Orange County he tried to apply its full rigor to a man who praised King George (1.191–92).

There was a touch of Robespierre in this young revolutionary. When Bradford reported from Philadelphia that there was talk of

Benjamin Franklin's secret ties to the monarchy, he responded that Franklin *must* be disloyal if he was not an active informer:

> Indeed it appears to me that the bare suspicion of his guilt amounts very nearly to a proof of its reality. If he were the man he formerly was, and has even of late pretended to be, his conduct in Philadelphia on this critical occasion could have left no room for surmise or distrust. He certainly would have been both a faithful informer and an active member of the Congress. His behavior would have been explicit and his zeal warm and conspicuous. We have a report here that [Theodoric] Bland, one of our delegates, has turned traitor and fled from Philadelphia. . . . Though appointed a member of Congress, Bland is in needy circumstances, and we all know age is not a stranger to avarice. (1.151–52)

He was as wrong about Bland as about Franklin. But he was willing to call into question even the loyalty of Washington (whom he had never met) for not joining Patrick Henry in an effort to recapture colonial powder taken by the British. Washington's loyalty was suspect because "gentlemen below [Madison's Piedmont], whose property will be exposed in case of a civil war in this colony, were extremely alarmed lest government should be provoked to make reprisals" (1.145). Madison's McCarthyite logic in these days (when he was in his early twenties) is summed up in his claim that "the times are so remarkable for strange events, that improbability is almost become an argument for their truth" (1.152). He displayed a paradox not rare in revolutions, an *authoritarian* rebelliousness. Some traces of this attitude lingered in his later conviction that Hamilton was a willing agent of England's king.

Madison's lifelong admiration of his father's plantation regimen dovetailed with his own great need for personal discipline, based on concern for his health. His early mentor and relative, Edmund Pendleton, referred to "your crazy [shattered] constitution" (3.172). Late in his life Madison told his biographer, William Cabell Rives, that he had "a constitutional liability to sudden attacks, somewhat resembling epilepsy and suspending the intellectual functions" (K 51). Modern medicine rules out epilepsy, but Madison clearly felt he had to maintain as strict a regimen over himself as his father did over his plantation. He lived to be eighty-five thanks to that regimen. And he was methodical in preparing his responses to situations beforehand, which meant that he rarely had to improvise on the spot. Even the rare breakdowns of his calm came from the high regard he had for order and stability. He was edgily impatient with those who disregarded or opposed social discipline. His impatience with the states that were not "doing their part" for the Revolution would be a good example of this.

RELIGION

The young Madison's self-restraint almost gave way on one subject. He wrote to William Bradford in 1774 (he was twenty-three): "I have neither patience to hear, talk, or think of anything relative to this matter, for I have squabbled and scolded, abused and ridiculed, so long about this, to so little purpose, that I am without common patience" (1.106). He was responding to the imprisonment of Baptist preachers by the established church in Virginia. His sense of order had been offended by the dissolute and idle Anglican clergy, by what he called "pride, ignorance, and knavery among the priesthood" (1.106). He contrasted these priests with the sincere and energetic Presbyterians he had met and admired while attending Princeton. The very reason he had left Virginia for his education was that the colony's own College of William and Mary was run by incompetent Anglicans. The teacher there who had been helpful to Jefferson, William Small, was gone by the time Madison was ready for college, and the school's revival, which would occur with Jefferson on its board, was still some way off in the future.

When the sixteen-year-old Madison finished five years of schooling with a respected Scottish "dominie," Donald Robertson, in King and Queen County, his father brought him back to Orange County for two years. He had reached the normal age for entering college, but James Senior kept him home to monitor his health, and brought in a tutor for him. Thomas Martin, a recent graduate of Princeton, recommended that his pupil go to his alma mater for completing his studies. This was a great boon to Madison, and to the country he would serve. John Witherspoon, from Scotland, was just finishing his first year as president of the college. He supplied his pupils with up-to-the-minute reports from the Scottish Enlightenment, which was at its peak of intellectual excitement. Madison's great respect for "the Doctor," as he always called Witherspoon, nearly equaled that for his father. Thanks to Madison's tutoring at home, he was able to finish the regular Princeton course in two years, but he stayed on for an extra year of private study with Witherspoon, who sent him back to Virginia with an ambitious program for further reading (1.89). Madison went into a period of private study that delayed his choice of any career until the Revolution pulled him from his cabinet.

Perhaps more important than the formal studies he completed at Princeton was the experience of a setting where religious freedom was practiced and defended. The school proposed to educate with "free and equal liberty and advantage of education any person of any religious denomination whatever" (K 30). Despite his patriotism toward Virginia, Madison had to admit that his own colony lacked the vital freedom of religious thought and practice. In his close circle of friends at the school were several who entered, or considered entering, the Presbyterian ministry, and he admired and kept in touch with them for years. They visited his father's plantation and were allowed to preach in the Anglican stronghold of Virginia (1.136). Madison even went to Philadelphia in 1774, when the Presbyterians' annual synod was taking place, to see the friends assembling there (1.113).

His Princeton experience was not limited to his three years' residence at the college (1769–72), since he kept up a correspondence with his classmates for years, and had important later dealings with some of them (like Philip Freneau). The Princeton/Presbyterian network was an overlay placed across the Virginia web of connections. The interaction in his mind of these apparently contradictory systems can be seen in the typically Virginian way Madison expressed Presbyterian values.

If the Church of England had been the established and general religion in all the northern colonies as it has been among us here, and uninterrupted tranquility had prevailed throughout the continent, it is clear to me that slavery and subjection might and would have been gradually insinuated among us. (1.105)

Like his peers, Madison uses a rhetoric of slavery totally unrelated to the real slaves he owned. For him, slavery meant any retrenchment of the rights he felt entitled to as a member of his ruling class. What made him different from many Virginians was that he included religious freedom among the rights his people deserved. It was a new item in an old category of privilege.

Only one of Madison's Princeton friends had the foresight to keep a register of their correspondence with Madison, but we are lucky that the one who did, William Bradford, lived in Philadelphia. Madison pestered him with repeated questions on the way religious disestablishment worked in Pennsylvania. He wanted a copy of the colonial charter, "a draft of its original and fundamental principles of legislation, particularly the extent of your religious toleration" (1.101). He congratulated Bradford on freedoms that Virginians did not enjoy, and asked him to "pity me and pray for liberty of conscience [in Virginia]." He was reaching one of his deepest convictions: "Religious bondage shackles and debilitates the mind and unfits it for every noble enterprise, every expanded prospect" (1.112–13).

When the twenty-five-year-old Madison was elected to the Virginia Convention, he demonstrated for the first time what would be his greatest strength in committee, prior preparation. The convention was drafting Virginia's trailblazing Declaration of Rights, under the guidance of its principal draftsman, George Mason. The article on religion said "that all men should enjoy the fullest toleration in the exercise of religion, according to the dictates of conscience." This was considered the liberal position, based on Locke's treatise on toleration; but Madison had already moved beyond it. His reflections on the contrast between Virginia's and Pennsylvania's systems had made him realize that the state has no right to "tolerate" the free exercise of conscience, any more than it has the right to limit that exercise. The proposal of this young little newcomer was written into law as Article XVI, asserting that "all men are equally entitled to the free exercise of religion according to the dictates of conscience

(1.175). Madison was defending a natural right, one (as he would later put it) "not within the cognizance of civil government" (8.301).

Madison's views on religious freedom are the inspiration for all that was best in his later political thought. This was the first subject to which he devoted his prodigious capacity for research and reflection. But private study was not the only factor in this brilliant legislative debut. In this case, his position grew out of actual experience—unlike some of his later schemes. The time at Princeton had disturbed one crucial aspect of his provincialism. He had *seen* the difference between Presbyterian divines in New Jersey and Anglican priests in Virginia. Some modern critics of Madison's separation of church from state think it is a "secularist" position, one that somehow downgrades or disables religion. On the contrary, he observed the greater sincerity of religious practice under conditions of freedom. This became a touchstone for him of the blessings of freedom in general. It was a religious insight before it was a political one. And his view has been vindicated in the history of the United States. Under our system, which separates church and state, religion has flourished more than in any modern industrialized society.

Because the bill for religious freedom that Madison would carry through to passage in 1785 worked from the original draft proposed by Jefferson in 1777, some think that Madison was just following Jefferson's lead. But his Article XVI was passed even before Jefferson proposed his bill, at a time when the young Madison had not even met Jefferson. The two men reached their convictions separately, and Madison would defend the concept of free conscience more extensively and effectively than even Jefferson ever did, when he composed *The Memorial and Remonstrance Against Religious Assessments* (8.298–304). He would also, of course, draft and steer to passage the First Amendment on religious freedom. As president, he defended that Amendment (as we shall see) by presidential vetoes. I do not want to take any credit away from Jefferson, who put his bill for religious freedom on his tombstone as one of his three greatest achievements. But the close association of the bill with Jefferson has taken some attention away from Madison's long labors in this cause, and to the centrality of it in his thinking. The more immediate point in this place is that the opening of his career marked Madison out as primarily a legislator. He did not aspire to be more than that. He knew its importance.

CONTINENTAL CONGRESS

After service on the Virginia governor's Council of State (1777–79), Madison was elected to the Continental Congress in 1779. He had envied his friend, William Bradford, who watched the first Continental Congress assemble in his hometown of Philadelphia. He asked for news of it, and wished he could be there (1.121). Now he was on his way to the arena where he would accomplish so much. As usual, he had done his homework. The difficulties of financing the Revolution, the inflation of paper money, and the states' non-delivery of requisitions from the Congress, were obviously going to be important matters considered in Congress. So Madison studied finance before leaving home, and wrote a little treatise, *Money*, to straighten out priorities in his own mind (1.302–9). Most of his fellow delegates had no idea what a formidable addition was being made to their assemblage. Madison was almost thirty, but he looked barely twenty. His combination of public diffidence and confidence in his research made people think him at once retiring and cocky. The wife of his fellow Virginian, Theodoric Bland, called him "a gloomy stiff creature," and Thomas Rodney of Delaware said he "possesses all the self-conceit that is common to youth and inexperience" (K 107).

But Madison's quiet committee work would soon compel attention and admiration, even where he could not command agreement. Congress was a fluid body. Even its location shifted about according to war conditions. It was hard to keep up a quorum. Sporadic and short attendance, one-year terms, and rotation out after three years, made it hard to assure continuity of attention and effective performance. Madison settled in for three years of hard work. His sense of order was outraged at the conditions he found when he arrived in Philadelphia. Writing a first report to his governor (Jefferson, not yet his intimate), he described the disorder in a long periodic sentence of classically balanced clauses, as if picking up the disgusting situation in tongs:

Our army threatened with an immediate alternative of disbanding or living on free quarter; the public treasury empty; public credit exhausted; nay, the private credit of purchasing agents employed, I am told, as far as it will bear; Congress complaining of the extortion of the people, the people of the improvidence of Congress, and the army of both; our affairs requiring the most mature and systematic measures, and the urgency of occasions admitting only of temporizing expedients, and those expedients generating new difficulties; Congress, from a defect of adequate statesmen, more likely to fall into wrong measures, and of less weight to enforce right ones; recommending plans to the several states for execution, and the states separately rejudging the expediency of such plans, whereby the same distrust of concurrent exertions that has damped the ardor of patriotic individuals must produce the same effect among the states themselves; an old system of finance discarded as incompetent to our necessities, an untried and precarious one substituted, and a total stagnation in prospect between the end of the former and the operation of the latter—these are the outlines of the true picture of our public situation. (2.6)

That is not the way his father ran the Madison plantation. It was clearly no way to run a Revolution. He was reminded daily of the runaway inflation by his boarding costs, which quickly passed what Congress was paying him. The cost for staying in a crowded boardinghouse during the first three months was twenty thousand dollars (2.253), and that rate would go up the longer he stayed in Philadelphia. His father, as usual, supplied him with funds; but he still had to borrow money, and by his third term he told his father that, unless Congress raised the delegates' pay, "I shall be under the necessity of selling a Negro" (4.127).[1]

Madison introduced order into many procedures. By his second term, however, things remained so desperate that a committee was asked to seek ways of getting the states to comply with congressional directives. Madison's personal frustration made him carry the committee with him in recommending a course that the larger body prudently shuffled off to death by further study. This was an extreme measure that Madison said was justified by the implied powers of the Articles of Confederation. But since it was impossible that this argument would be accepted, he called for an amendment to the Articles declaring

> that the said United States in Congress assembled are fully authorized to employ the force of the United States, as well by sea as by land, to compel such state or states to fulfill their federal engagements, and particularly to make distraint [seizure] on any of the effects, vessels, and merchandises of such state or states, or of any of the citizens thereof, wherever found; and to prohibit and prevent their trade and inter-course, as well with any other of the United States and the citizens thereof as with any foreign state, and as well by land as by sea, until full compensation or compliance be obtained with respect of all requisitions made by the United States in Congress assembled, in pursuance of the Articles of Confederation. (3.18)

Those last three words are a bit of bravado, since the powers asked for were deliberately denied in the Articles. The amazing thing is that Madison would even bother to propose this as an amendment, since amendments to the Articles required a unanimous vote of the states, and the possibility of getting even one state to vote for this measure, much less all of the states, was simply nil.

Yet Madison refused to abandon his plan. It became an idée fixe with him. He argued its practicability to Governor Jefferson. Madison showed how little he knew this man, at this stage, when he calmly proposed things that were anathema to traditional Whigs— a standing army (Whigs wanted only militia), and a permanent navy (Whigs wanted only privateers):

> The *necessity* of arming Congress with coercive powers arises from the shameful deficiency of some of the states which are most capable of yielding their apportioned supplies. . . . *Without such powers*, too, in the general government, the whole confederacy may be insulted [assailed] and the most salutary measure frustrated . . . as the confederation now

stands, and according to the nature even of alliances much
less intimate, there is an implied *right of coercion* against the
delinquent party, and the exercise of it by Congress, when-
ever a palpable necessity occurs, will *probably be acquiesced
in.* . . . It may be asked perhaps by what means Congress
could exercise such a power if the states were to invest them
with it? As long as there is a *regular army on foot*, a small
detachment from it, acting under civil authority, would at any
time render a voluntary [*sic*] contribution for supplies due
from a state an eligible [desirable] alternative. But there is a
still more *easy and efficacious* mode. The situation of most of
the states is such that two or three *vessels of force*, employed
against their trade, will make it their interest to yield prompt
obedience to all just requisitions on them. With respect to
those states that have little or no foreign trade of their own, it
is provided that all inland trade with such states as supply
them with foreign merchandise may be interdicted, and the
concurrence of the latter may be *enforced*, in case of refusal,
by operation on their *foreign* trade. (3.72, emphasis added)

That last sentence is breathtaking in its scope. Madison would use
federal armed force to punish a coastal state for refusing to cooperate in the punishment of an inland state. One might think there was
no fantasy Madison would not entertain in his irritation at the
recalcitrant states. And in fact he goes on to claim that this amendment would provide a long-term bonus by forcing the confederacy
to develop a navy, since that would be a postwar instrument of
national unity:

> There is a collateral reason, which interests the states who are
> feeble in maritime resources, in such a plan. If a naval arma-
> ment was considered as the proper instrument of general gov-
> ernment, it would be both preserved in a respectable state in
> time of peace, and it would be an object to man it with citi-
> zens taken in due proportion from every state. (3.72)

We read those words, now, with a knowledge that Madison would
later support President Jefferson's hostility to a navy *precisely* as an

instrument of national purpose. It would be unfair to hold him to consistency on this single issue. But the whole proposal for this enforcement power is interesting to a student of his presidency—as part of a pattern that will be repeated. Madison could become so attached to what seemed to him the obvious *appropriateness* of a plan that he lost all sight of its *practicability*. We shall see the same thing happen in his drafting of the Constitution and of the Bill of Rights, and in policies he supported during Jefferson's and his own administrations as president.

In all these cases, a characteristic of Madison is the naive insistence on proposals that had no chance of being adopted. In 1785, he was still arguing in the Virginia Assembly for what he had proposed four years before in Congress. He continued to claim that coercion of the states would be feasible and "easy," once one made coastal states punish inland ones. All that was required was

a recognition by the states of the authority of Congress to enforce payment of their respective quotas . . . the use of coercion, or such provision as would render the use of it unnecessary, might be made at little expense and [in] perfect safety. A single frigate, under the orders of Congress, could make it the interest of any one of the Atlantic states to pay its just quota. With regard to such of the ultramontane states as depend on the trade of the Mississippi, as small a force would have the same effect; whilst the residue, trading through the Atlantic states, might be wrought upon by means more indirect, indeed, but perhaps sufficiently effectual. (8.374)

2

The Constitution
(1786–1788)

The use of term limits was widespread during the Revolution, where they demonstrated their impracticality. Because of them, Madison, one of the most valuable and conscientious members of the Continental Congress, had to leave it in 1783—he had served his limit of three one-year terms. Some modern advocates of term limits say they want to prevent elected people from becoming professional politicians, rather than citizens doing public service for short periods. If that was the aim in the eighteenth century, it certainly failed. Madison, like most of those rotated out of office, remained a politician, just moving to a different office—in his case, to the Virginia House of Delegates in 1784. This is where he passed the bill for religious freedom, mentioned earlier in connection with his Presbyterian ties.

Even while serving as part of the Virginia legislature in Richmond, Madison maintained contact with his state's delegates in the Continental Congress. He still hoped to strengthen Congress by amending the Articles. He opposed several efforts to go outside that process, since he thought they would further dilute the already-thin powers of Congress. That is why he was lukewarm when his fellow delegate in the Virginia Assembly, John Tyler, called in 1785 for a meeting at Annapolis to consider means of regulating commerce (8.406–9). This 1786 meeting at Annapolis, to which he was sent as a delegate, might have been expected to confirm his doubts, since it could move nothing for lack of a quorum (9.115–19). But Madison, Hamilton, and others decided to use it for summoning a larger convention, to consider amending the Articles.

THE CONSTITUTIONAL CONVENTION

Madison left Annapolis an ardent convert to the idea of a convention. He stopped off at Mount Vernon to recruit Washington to the proposal—it was the beginning of a long wooing process that would finally break down Washington's reluctance to leave Mount Vernon. Madison had completed his three years of rotation out from the Continental Congress, and he returned to it now with a determination to head off any objections to the convention. Congress authorized the meeting, but *only* for proposing amendments to the Articles (which, remember, required ratification by *all* the states in the confederation). By now, Madison had larger purposes in mind— and that was clear to Washington, who realized that if anything effectual were to be done, it would have to break the terms of the Articles.[1] Among the many reasons Washington had for resisting the project, this was the greatest—it would involve its participants in the breaking of their oaths of allegiance to the Articles. That was—in one plausible interpretation of what they were up to— treason. We call the meeting in Philadelphia, retrospectively, the Constitutional Convention, since it produced a new constitution. Its participants could not have called it that, since they could not admit they were up to any such nefarious business. While the meeting was being held, "the constitution" was still the word regularly used for the Articles. What they were holding was really an *anti*constitutional convention.

If other delegates, less clearheaded than Washington, showed up at Philadelphia in 1787 unaware of the meeting's subversive nature, they had a rude awakening when Edmund Randolph presented the "Virginia Plan" for consideration. This was based on a draft by Madison, and it recommended abrogation of the Articles, not amendment of them. For a start, it proposed that a new constitution must be ratified by special conventions, not by state legislatures (the only means allowed under the Articles). Even more stunning, the federal government would be empowered to veto laws passed by state legislatures, a denial of the state sovereignty expressly reserved in the Articles (10.16–17). The pretense that this was a plan to "correct" the Articles was transparently false. The convention had to go into secret session, and remain there for its whole time of meeting. It even had to move to the second floor of the State House, so no one could overhear what they were doing. (Some popular accounts err when they have the tense debates take place in the downstairs legislative chamber, with the windows wide open.) If the state legislatures that had sent these delegates found out what was going on, they would have recalled them for breaking their instructions.

Against a drumbeat of criticism directed at "the dark conclave," Washington himself, as presiding officer, strictly monitored the secrecy provision until the final document was released, and the delegates scuttled nervously away from the scene of the crime. Critics of the document were probably right when they said that the members of the convention would have been denounced for treason had not "great names" given them cover—Franklin's name and, especially, Washington's. It would take great temerity to call *them* enemies of their country. One of Madison's greatest services to America was his help in ensuring Washington's attendance at the convention. He negotiated the matter with great delicacy. When Washington turned down a first request that he attend, Madison cooperated with Edmund Randolph (then the governor of Virginia) to appoint the general as leader of the Virginia delegation. He urged Washington, even if he did not plan to accept the offer, not to reject it immediately, in case some emergency should arise that would make him reconsider (9.224). Madison knew that if Washington's name were standing as the presumed head of delegation, that might convince other states that this was a serious endeavor. If this ploy did not work, the convention would be called off, and Washington would not have committed himself to a failure. If, on the other hand, other states came aboard (and Madison was working in Congress to bring that about), this fact could be reported to Washington as a spur for his attendance (9.315).

In drawing up the Virginia Plan, Madison made another of his careful preparations before any deliberative session. It was the most important study he ever made. Historian Douglass Adair called his work in the spring of 1787 "probably the most fruitful piece of scholarly research ever carried out by an American."[2] In order to criticize the Articles, Madison isolated the category they belonged to, the "confederation" as a league or an alliance, and then surveyed history to show how sorry was the performance of such leagues—we know this survey as "Notes on Ancient and Modern Confederacies" (9.3–24). Then, having established the faults of the type, he applied his findings to the specific example, in "Vices of the Political System of the United States" (9.345–57).

The main problem with a confederacy is the fact that its components remain sovereign, so there is no single center of decision, and no way for that center to enforce its authority:

> A sanction is essential to the idea of law, as coercion is to that of the government. The federal system, being destitute of both, wants the great vital principles of a political constitution. Under the forms of such a constitution, it is in fact nothing more than a treaty of amity or commerce, and of alliance between so many independent and sovereign states. (9.351)

We have been returned to Madison's favorite idea of the time, that of coercing the states, but no longer in a wartime context, not as punishment for lagging revolutionaries but as part of a fixed system. This is the study that led him to the most daring proposal in his plan, giving "the national legislature" authority

> to legislate *in all cases* to which the separate states are incompetent, or in which the harmony of the United States may be interrupted by the exercise of individual legislation; to negative *all* laws, passed by the several states, contravening, *in the opinion of the national legislature*, the articles of union; and to call for the force of the union against any member of the union failing to fulfill its duty under the articles thereof. (20.26, emphasis added)

Some have tried to minimize this call for central power, saying it was to be used only defensively by the national legislature, to fend off invasions of its authority. If that were the case, Madison should have stopped after the second clause above; but he went on to say that *all* laws fall under this power, with no norm but the *opinion* (judgment) of the national legislature. He was an experienced enough legislator to know that this was no way to frame a *limited* power.

Writing to Washington before the convention, Madison did not propose the veto as limited by anything but the good sense of its wielder: "A negative *in all cases whatsoever* on the legislative acts of the states, as heretofore exercised by the kingly prerogative, appears to me to be absolutely necessary" (9.383, emphasis in Madison's original). He had already made the same point to Jefferson, saying that he meant "to arm the federal head with a negative *in all cases whatsoever* on the local legislatures" (9.318, emphasis in the original).[3] In the convention itself he used language not at all suggesting strict limits, describing "an *indefinite* power to negative legislative acts of the states as *absolutely necessary* to a perfect [complete] system" (10.41, emphasis added). To Washington he argued that such a veto might preclude the use of naked force against the states:

> The right of coercion should be expressly declared. With the resources of commerce in hand, the national administration might always find means of exerting it, either by sea or land. But the difficulty and awkwardness of operating by force on the collective will of a state render it particularly desirable that the necessity for it might be precluded. Perhaps the negative on the laws might create such a mutuality of dependence between the general and particular authorities as to answer this purpose. (9.385)

In the debates of the convention, Madison argued that the veto was the most important part of his plan, comparing it to gravity in the Newtonian cosmos:

> To recur to the illustrations borrowed from the planetary system, this prerogative of the general government is the great pervading principle that must control the centrifugal tendency of the states, which without it will continually fly out of their proper orbits and destroy the whole harmony of the political system. (10.41)

When the convention failed to adopt this central point in his plan, Madison feared that the new government could not succeed. Writing to Jefferson five weeks after the convention adjourned, he said:

Without such a check in the whole over the parts, our system involves the evil of *imperia in imperio* [sovereignties within a sovereignty]. If a complete supremacy somewhere is not necessary in every society, a controlling power at least is so. . . . The case of the United Netherlands is in point. The authority of a Statholder, the influence of a standing army, the common interests in the conquered possessions, the pressure of surrounding danger, the guarantee of foreign powers, are not sufficient to secure the authority and interests of the generality against the antifederal tendency of the provincial sovereignties. (9.209–10)

There was never the slightest hope that the states would ratify a scheme with that provision. A very hard fight was needed to pass the document, by a narrow margin, even without this provocative item. The mere knowledge that it had been seriously proposed and discussed might have been enough to sink the whole project. This is another case where secrecy proved necessary to the treasonous project of giving us our Constitution

THE FEDERALIST

When Madison left the Constitutional Convention, he had to decide whether to return to Congress, which was sitting in New York. There was a good chance that there would be no quorum for that teetering body, now that the action had moved outside its orbit; and friends in Virginia were urging Madison to begin the work of ratifying in their state. But he might also have to protect the draft in Congress, so he felt obliged to travel north (after stopping off to coordinate plans with Washington at Mount Vernon). It is fortunate that he did. If he had not, Hamilton would not have turned to him for help in the great series of newspaper articles he had launched, and *The Federalist* as we know it would not exist.

Hamilton's series, written under the collective pseudonym "Publius" (the Public Man), was a targeted act of propaganda. He meant to turn out a rapid defense of the Constitution, point by point, in time to influence the election of delegates to the New York ratifying convention. This would have to be a joint effort, to produce the essays in time for their purpose. In this immediate aim, the series failed. Before it could be completed, a majority opposed to the Constitution was elected for the convention. (New York eventually ratified, but with provisos and *faute de mieux*, as it became clear that other states would go on without New York if it rejected the draft.) Hamilton meant for Publius to be a team of New Yorkers addressing New Yorkers—John Jay, William Duer, and Gouverneur Morris (born in New York, though not living there). Morris turned him down, Duer produced some essays that were rejected as inadequate, and Jay began to collaborate but was prevented by illness from making a large contribution.

To Hamilton's relief, Madison turned up in New York just in time to take up this joint labor with him. Madison was not a New Yorker, but the shared pseudonym would not betray that fact—and Madison wrote nothing to betray a southern, much less a Virginian, perspective. Publius presented himself as a mere interested New Yorker, one who had not taken part in the framing of the draft or in any official role at all. Hamilton expected (and received) general agreement from Madison, since they had been allies at every stage of the effort to change the Articles. Madison, in order to perform as Publius, did not have to repress disagreement with Hamilton, but with the draft itself. He could not mention his regret that the veto on state laws was not included. In fact, he would go out of his way to assuage state anxieties. He also made the best of the fact that the states were equally represented in the Senate, a provision he had strenuously opposed in Philadelphia. Once recruited, Madison took up the joint effort with a will, lingering in New York to complete twenty-nine of the eighty-five Numbers (as they were called).

The first nine Numbers, written by Hamilton and Jay before Madison's arrival, described the failure of the Articles. Madison's debut contribution, Number 10, would in time (a long time) become the most famous of them all. It crammed into a narrow space all the arguments Madison had been sifting and refining in his opposition to the Continental Congress's weakness, in his preparation for the convention, in his crafting of the Virginia Plan, and in his debates at the convention. Madison goes behind specific weaknesses in the Articles to expose the fundamental error on which the Articles were based, the idea that the only worthy democracy is direct democracy.

Madison's attack on that concept is so radical for its time that it is often downplayed, or even altogether missed. The most important passage in the Number is its claim that no man can be a judge in his own case. Not much is made of that in some treatments of the Number. We hear about the tyranny of majorities (though Madison treats that as just a symptom of direct democracy). We hear about the difference between a small republic and an extended republic (whereas Madison is talking about the difference between a direct democracy and a republic). We hear that Madison wanted to multiply factions (though he thought all factions bad things). We hear that Madison wanted to create a national elite, above the states, because he distrusted the people (though his system calls precisely for trust—direct democracy is built on distrust). We hear that he was trying to set up a mechanical system for producing correct decisions (though he said that no governmental machinery can produce good results without virtue in it operators).

It has puzzled people that Number 10 did not get much attention until the twentieth century. It was not a matter of great dispute in the ratification debates, though it would have clarified and focused those debates—they spent endless hours on the *number* of representatives, rather than on the *nature* of representation. The reason for this is that a dismissal of direct democracy was almost literally unthinkable to the men who debated the Constitution. Every constitution in America was based on that ideal, as a thing to be approximated even when it could not be literally enacted. If people could not directly make the government's decisions, as in a New England town meeting or the Athenian Assembly, then they should tie down those making the decisions, making them (so far as possible) passive tools in their own hands. That is why short terms, rotation, instruction, open proceedings (to see that instruction is followed), recall (to punish departures from instruction), and weak executives were adopted. These were the necessary melioratives for the necessary evil of any departure from direct democracy.

The rightness of all these measures was so self-evident to those who accepted them that they could not even imagine someone making the attack on them that Madison did. He did not say, as many did, that direct democracy would be wonderful if it were possible but, since it is not possible in large communities, some approximation to it must be cobbled up. He did not think direct democracy wonderful. He thought it fundamentally unjust.

No man is allowed to be a judge in his own cause, because his interests would certainly bias his judgment, and, not improbably, corrupt his integrity. With equal, nay with greater reason, a body of men are unfit to be both judges and parties at the same time; yet what are many of the most important acts of legislation but so many *judicial* determinations, not indeed concerning the right of single persons but concerning the right of large bodies of citizens; and what are the different classes of legislators but advocates and parties to the causes which they determine? (10.266, emphasis added)

By calling legislation quasi-judicial, he instantly disqualifies all those who come to the task of legislating with nothing but their own interest in mind. They have come to be judges in their own case—and that is what proponents of direct democracy would justify. In doing so, they defend a system of majority tyranny. If naked interest is all that can be expressed, then only one thing will determine the outcome. The only question to be decided is: which interest has the greater number backing it.

Is a law proposed concerning private debts? It is a question to which the creditors are parties on one side, and the debtors on the other. Justice ought to hold the balance between them. Yet the parties are and must be themselves the judges; and the most numerous party, or in other words, the most powerful faction, must be expected to prevail. Shall domestic manufactures be encouraged, and in what degree, by restrictions on foreign manufactures, are questions that will be differently decided by the landed and the manufacturing classes; and probably by neither with a sole regard to justice and the public good. The apportionment of taxes on the various descriptions of property is an act which seems to require the most exact impartiality; yet there is perhaps no legislative action in which greater opportunity and temptation are given to a predominant party to trample on the rules of justice. Every shilling with which they overburden the inferior number is a shilling saved to their own pockets. (10.266)

Madison thought that government should be essentially arbitrative, with neutral umpires weighing competing interests, to strike a just balance. Resort to arbiters was a regular practice among Virginians, and it shows that the issue was not simply distrust of others. In 1790, when Jefferson bought a horse from Madison, he feared that his friend would not demand a fair price, so he suggested a trusted arbiter: "I propose your getting a Captain Wood or some such good judge to do you justice" (J 17.512). When the horse died, Madison suggested an arbiter to decide whether Jefferson should be held to the original price—"a common friend should hear and decide the case" (January 11, 1791). Washington recommended and practiced this procedure in setting prices. The Articles of Confederation, since it lacked a sitting judiciary, prescribed a system of arbitration for legal conflicts.

But where was one to get neutral arbiters for the governing of whole communities? Earlier polities, like medieval Siena, had solved this problem by bringing in foreign judges to carry out the city's functions impartially.[4] Madison wanted to achieve that end without resort to such exotic means. This meant separating the officials, in some measure, from their local ties, freeing them to be impartial ("indifferent"). That is why the Constitution gives elected officials long terms (relative to expectations at the time), no rotation, no recall. That is why representatives are paid from federal funds, not from the state treasuries as if employed by them. In an extended sphere, moreover, where the representatives both traveled from their base and met a broad mixture of other regions' spokesmen, conditions would encourage men to adjudicate matters on their merit. The motive for choosing a man of probity to bargain with others would be the same as if Madison and Jefferson were choosing a mutually acceptable arbiter to set the price on a horse. The electors would already be balancing their interest against their regard for justice in choosing such a person. In that sense, a republic is a school of virtue—as opposed to direct democracy, where the representatives must be slaves to the interests of those sending them.

Another advantage of an extended sphere is that the districts voting must be made comparatively large, in order to keep the representatives comparatively few—or the national assembly would be unmanageably overpopulated. This ensures not only that there is a larger pool to choose from, but that a complex weave of interests, not a single one, would be in play during this first step, of sending representatives to meet their peers.

Madison had experience backing up this theoretical position. When he went to the Continental Congress, he was impressed by many of those he met and he learned to cooperate with people from other regions, to support things not envisaged by those who elected him—as when he worked with Hamilton to strengthen the Articles, and then to supplant them. Even when he resented the agents of other interests, as in the case of Virginia's cession of western lands to Congress, he had to compromise with their interests, and he came in time to see some of the reasons behind them. In dealing with foreign representatives in Philadelphia (especially La Luzerne, the Frenchman resented by some of his constituents), he also learned to assess new points of view. In order to foster that same ability, he justified the Constitution's long term for senators— they would have time to acquire experience in dealing with foreign attitudes. In this, senators would both earn and show respect for other countries:

> Without a select and stable member of the government, the esteem of foreign powers will not only be forfeited by an unenlightened and variable policy, proceeding from the causes already mentioned, but the national councils will not possess that sensibility to the opinion of the world which is perhaps not less necessary in order to merit than it is to obtain its respect and confidence. An attention to the judgment of other nations is important to every government for two reasons. The one is that, independently of the merits of any particular plan or measure, it is desirable on various

accounts that it should appear to other nations as the off-spring of a wise and honorable policy. The second is that, in doubtful cases, particularly where the national councils may be warped by some strong passion or momentary interest, the presumed or known opinion of the impartial world may be the best guide that can be followed. (10.544)

Those words from *The Federalist* Number 63, the last one he wrote, are appropriate because he stayed on in New York to finish his last essays, even after Congress had adjourned. Then he had to rush down to Virginia, where he defended the draft at his own state's ratifying convention. The words he wrote in Number 63 are a key to his effort in Richmond, since their description of international deliberation applies, mutatis mutandis, to domestic bargaining by representatives in an extended republic, who must come to grips with the views of those from other regions.

RATIFICATION IN VIRGINIA

Madison's friends feared that he had delayed too long to rescue the Constitution's prospects in Virginia. Patrick Henry had mobilized his considerable skills and connections to defeat the draft. Even Madison's warmest supporters knew he was not in Henry's class as a public orator—and Henry had George Mason with him, along with much of the state's planter aristocracy. Jefferson, writing from Paris, feared that, though Madison would be the main supporter, and "an immensely powerful one, it is questionable whether he can bear the weight of such a host" (J 12.425). Henry played expertly on the fears of sending a representative off to a distant place, without the clogs of short terms, instruction, recall, and so on. Those were the only real checks on power. To trust a representative to defend the state's interest without those controls was not in human nature.

It is often said that the Constitution, and Madison as its framer, expressed a pessimistic view of human nature, as something that cannot be trusted with power. That would more aptly describe Patrick Henry. Madison claimed, on the contrary, that republican virtue is precisely the willingness to let a disinterested spokesman do all he can do for one's interest *in an arena of just arbitration.*

When Washington and his fellow Virginians chose an arbiter to settle disputes, they were relying on a code of gentlemen; but Madison said that ordinary citizens can rise above narrow interest, trusting their delegates to make the best bargain for them, in conjunction with the just claims of others:

> I go on this great republican principle, that the people will have virtue and intelligence to select men of virtue and wisdom. Is there no virtue among us? If there be not, we are in a wretched situation. No theoretical check, no form of government, can render us secure. To suppose that any form of government will secure liberty or happiness without any virtue in the people is a chimerical idea. If there be sufficient virtue and intelligence in the community, it will be exercised in the selection of these men, so that we do not depend on their virtue, or put confidence in our rulers, but in the people who are to choose them.[5]

Good as Henry was as an orator and debater, he was not a reflective or studious person, and he was up against a man who had thought and debated and persuaded on this subject through two years that sharpened all of Madison's analytical power and parliamentary deftness. The tiny David slew the mighty Goliath.

A neglected aspect of this dramatic confrontation is the effect it had on a young lawyer sitting among the delegates, John Marshall. Listening for days to Madison carefully unfold the inmost meaning of the Constitution, Marshall was, in effect, being given a tutorial or seminar on the subject that would absorb most of his adult life. Similarly, at the Constitutional Convention, the nature of our government was being determined in the weeks while Washington listened intently as Madison explained the meaning of republican government. Washington was so convinced that Madison was the authoritative interpreter of the Constitution that, at the beginning of his presidency, he consulted the younger man on all his precedent-setting early moves. Marshall, too, as chief justice of the Supreme Court, would often be following Madison's arguments (though Madison would at times not recognize them, given his own divagations from what he held in the 1780s).

Madison is called the father of the Constitution. It is a title deeply deserved, on many counts. In the amazing time that stretched from the Annapolis Convention (September 1786) to the Virginia ratification (June 1788)—from his own thirty-fifth year to his thirty-seventh—he defended the Annapolis call to the Constitutional Convention in Congress, helped persuade Washington to attend it, did his research into the nature of confederacies, drafted the Virginia Plan, played a key role in transforming that plan into the finished draft, defended that draft in Congress and in *The Federalist*, and then returned to Richmond where he defeated Henry and won his state's ratification.

All this was accomplished by a man who had to move with a cautious regard for his "crazy constitution." He was able to do it because he had steeped himself in constitutional issues from the time when, at age twenty-two, he wrote to his friend in Philadelphia, who was commencing the study of law:

> The principles and modes of government are too important to be disregarded by an inquisitive mind, and I think are well worthy of a critical examination by all students that have health and leisure. I should be well pleased with a sketch of the plan you have fixed upon for your studies, the books and the order you intend to read them in; and when you have obtained sufficient insight into the constitution of your country, and can make it an amusement to yourself, send me a draft of its origin and fundamental principles of legislation. (1.101)

We can now read into those words (what he could not at the time) a high vocation, or even a personal destiny, to become a supremely great legislator.

Three Administrations
(1789-1809)

Madison, the fourth president of the United States, had an intimate connection with all three of the preceding administrations. He served in government throughout the two-term presidencies—as congressional leader during Washington's administration and as secretary of state during Jefferson's. Though he was out of the federal government during the one-term presidency of John Adams, he worked closely with the vice president of that administration, his friend Jefferson. He was also responsible for the most signal achievement of the new government, the framing and passage of the Bill of Rights.

After prevailing in the ratification struggle in Richmond, Madison went back to New York, to take up again his duties in Congress. This dumbfounded his Virginia allies, who thought there could be little going on there—they wanted him to stand for election as senator in the new Congress of the Constitution. But Madison refused to put himself forward—he preferred to serve in the House, election to which had to wait on the establishment of congressional districts. Washington feared that Henry would send Anti-Federalists to the Senate, who would call for a new convention to rewrite or amend the Constitution (Virginia's House of Delegates had voted for that). He urged Madison to run for the Senate and Madison complied, but too late to win the race (11.309–10). Henry had sewn up both Senate positions for his chosen men—he said Madison considered the Constitution perfect, and would not consider a new convention to improve it.

For elections to the House, Henry drew up the congressional districts in such a way as to weaken Madison's base in Orange County (Lance Banning calls it "Henrymandering").[1] He also persuaded James Monroe to run against Madison. In order to counter Henry's tactics, Madison had to promise that he would himself introduce amendments (though he had opposed that in Philadelphia and Richmond): "Amendments, if pursued with a proper moderation and in a proper mode, will be not only safe but may serve the double purpose of satisfying the minds of well-meaning opponents and of providing additional guards in favor of liberty" (11.404–5). Elected on that campaign promise, Madison observed it as his first matter of business in the new House of Representatives. He moved the passage of nineteen amendments. Those that passed the House and Senate were sent to the states, which ratified the ten known as the Bill of Rights. These included, of course, the guarantee of religious freedom in the First Amendment, a cause dear to Madison.

The amendments protect rights from violation by the federal government. We know that Madison wanted the disestablishment of religion guaranteed at the state level, as it was in Virginia. In fact, he wanted all the rights of conscience protected from state activity. This was the subject of the fourteenth in his original list of nineteen proposed amendments: "No state shall violate the equal rights of conscience, or the freedom of the press, or the trial by jury in criminal case" (12.202). This guarantee of the rights of conscience at the state level would have "federalized" much of the Bill of Rights long before that was accomplished in the twentieth century. Madison was returning to a theme he had sounded in the Constitutional Convention and in the documents prepared beforehand—that the states were at least as likely (he thought more likely) to deprive people of rights as was the federal government. Since the federal government would be enforcing these limits on the states, this move was a return to his call in Philadelphia for a veto on unjust state laws. When his proposed amendment was criticized because some states already had their own bills of rights, he answered that not all of them did; and, besides,

I cannot see any reason against obtaining even a double security on those points, and nothing can give a more sincere
proof of the attachment of those who opposed this Constitution to these great and important rights than to see them join
in obtaining the security I have now proposed; because it
must be admitted on all hands that the state governments are
as liable to attack the invaluable privileges as the general government is, and therefore ought to be as cautiously guarded
against. (12.208)

As he had with his veto on state laws at the Constitutional Convention, Madison emphasized the importance of the proposal, and
fought for it energetically. But restricting the states is hardly what
the Anti-Federalists had in mind when they called for a federal bill
of rights. In fact many of those who wanted to add a bill of rights to
the Philadelphia draft (including Patrick Henry himself) opposed
Madison's amendments—and not only because of the original fourteenth item (which was killed in the Senate before others on the
list were submitted to the states). They said that Madison had not
addressed their real concerns—abolishing the standing army from
Article I, restoring some of the direct checks like shorter terms, and
changing the ratios of apportionment. Those who construe the
Second Amendment (on the right of militias to bear arms) in the
Anti-Federalists' sense have to explain why the Anti-Federalists
themselves rejected it.

PRESIDENT WASHINGTON (1789-1797)

As Washington, at the Constitutional Convention, watched Madison steer the Constitution from conception to completed draft, he
sized him up and realized that no one else understood the nature of
the new enterprise better than this unimpressive little man with
libraries in his brain. When Washington was faced with the responsibility of translating the paper scheme into an operating government, he was conscious that every act of his was setting a
precedent, putting the executive on courses that would be hard to
redirect or eliminate. Since he meant to stay entirely true to the
genius of this particular republic, he consulted with Madison on

almost every aspect of his awesome assignment—choosing personnel, receiving ambassadors, addressing Congress, meeting with the
public. Madison deserves some of the credit that goes to Washington as the rare (perhaps unique) revolutionary leader who established a firm authority without overstepping its limits.

But by the end of Washington's second term, it was Madison who
was distorting the Constitution, exceeding his own authority, and
trying to tear down what he had helped build up. The climax of this
process was reached in 1796, during the conflict over the Jay Treaty
with England. Madison despised the terms of that treaty and the
process by which it was negotiated. So did Jefferson; but he was out
of the government by then, having resigned as secretary of state. It
was up to Madison, in the House of Representatives, to kill the
treaty, even though it had been ratified by the Senate and confirmed
by King George. That was the legal process Madison himself had
defined and defended, when he wrote *Federalist* Numbers 62 and 63
on the prerogatives of the Senate. The Senate, he said, was the
proper part of Congress to handle foreign affairs, confirming treaties
and ambassadors. It was qualified for this by its longer tenure, indirect election, and staggered terms—only it had the institutional
memory to provide a stable partner for other nations to trust.

Jefferson agreed with Madison at the time of the convention.
The popularly elected branch should handle money matters, but
not foreign affairs:

> I like the power given the legislature [House] to levy taxes;
> and for that reason solely approve of the greater [larger]
> house being chosen by the people directly. For though I think
> a house chosen by them [the people] will be *very illy qualified
> for [affairs of] the union, for foreign nations, etc.*, yet this evil
> does not weigh against the good of preserving inviolate the
> fundamental principle that the people are not to be taxed
> but by representatives chosen immediately by themselves.
> (10.336, emphasis added)

But Jefferson now welcomed anything that would kill the treaty:
"I trust the popular branch of our legislature will disapprove of it,
and thus rid us of this infamous act" (J 8.200). He now called the

constitutional process itself a party maneuver, "an attempt of a party which finds they have lost their majority in one branch of the legislature [the House] to make a law by the aid of the other branch and of the executive" (16.88). If the treaty were allowed to stand, treaty-making will be reserved to "the President, Senate, and Piarningo or any other Indian, Algerine or other chief" (RL 891). How to justify this change in position? Since the House controls money, Madison seized on the fact that commissions for arbitrating aspects of the treaty's settlement would need funding.

But that, of itself, would not cancel the treaty, just hamper its operation. So Madison went further. He backed the House in a demand that Washington send it the documentary record of how the treaty was negotiated. He and his fellows hoped to find evidence that a corrupt influence had been brought to bear. He was claiming a power in the House to nullify treaties after their ratification by the Senate. This was more than "loose construction" of the Constitution. It amounted to reversal of its plain sense. Madison was so angry at the Senate for its ratification that he praised the "firm example" given by the Virginia Assembly's proposal to shorten the Senate's terms to three years and strip it of powers including the trial of impeachments (16.170)—though Madison had previously supported six-year terms and wanted to *strengthen* the impeachment power.

It was time for Washington to read Madison a lesson on constitutionalism. He possessed the minutes of the Constitutional Convention, turned over to him for safekeeping at the end of its sessions. It was hoped that opponents of the Constitution would not have the temerity to demand the record from him, looking for ammunition during the ratifying process. Madison wanted to protect that record from the very kind of search he was now making into the Jay negotiations. But Washington felt free to quote the minutes, since the ratification crisis had passed. He turned all the minutes over to the State Department, for anyone to check his citation from them. That citation showed that the convention had specifically voted against the idea that ordinary legislation could reach to treaty-making (both Madison and Washington had voted with the majority against that claim).

Madison's allies looked to him to refute Washington from the record—he was, after all, an initiate to what had happened in Philadelphia. But Madison had always opposed making the convention proceedings public. He had good reason not to want people to know that he had strenuously worked for a federal veto on state laws. That position would always have been embarrassing to him, and it was particularly dangerous now, when he was supporting state measures like the Virginia motion to cut back the Senate's power. He kept his own notes from the convention secret all his lifetime, and he considered it a breach of confidence for Washington to have turned the official minutes over to the public (16.286). He claimed (erroneously) that Hamilton, now in private law practice in New York, must have put Washington up to this "improper and indelicate" act (16.286).

Washington won this battle on a constitutional issue, as the vote went against Madison in his own arena of the House, "a stunning Madisonian defeat."[2] Washington would never rely on him again, never consult him, never invite him to a private meeting in the executive mansion where Madison had been the trusted confidant, never receive him at Mount Vernon, where he had spent so many days and nights, regularly stopping off on trips to and from his home in Orange County. As the historian of their relationship puts it, Washington "washed his hands of his friend after the treaty affair."[3] He had concluded, after a long sad experience, that Madison was duplicitous and dishonorable.

How had things reached this point? There had been a mounting series of conflicts between Madison and Hamilton, conflicts in which Washington consistently sided with Hamilton. Madison proposed a tariff for revenue that would discriminate against British shipping—the principal source of United States revenue (K 280). Hamilton's allies defeated it. Hamilton had proposed redemption of continental paper emissions at face value—Madison wanted face value only for original holders, and what it had cost for secondary holders (13.41), a scheme that would have involved "big government" investigation and expense. Hamilton had proposed that the federal government assume all state war debts—Madison wanted them assumed as they stood at the end of the war (13.95), another more expensive procedure. Hamilton had proposed a national bank;

Madison opposed it (13.373–81). Hamilton had supported Washington's neutrality proclamation—Madison thought the president had no right to issue it, and that, by abandoning revolutionary France, "it wounds the popular feelings by a seeming indifference to the cause of liberty" (15.33). Even after the proclamation was issued, Madison accepted honorary French citizenship (RL 778), though Washington and Hamilton both turned down the same offer from the French government (B 4.458). Hamilton was happy with Washington's criticism of the democratic societies that supported the Whiskey Rebellion—Madison thought the criticism an assault on the First Amendment (15.397). Over and over in these conflicts, Madison lost in the arenas that mattered, in the executive mansion, in the Senate, even in his own House.

Madison tended to think that those who opposed what seemed to him the obvious truth must have evil motives. When the evil motives prevailed over a whole range of engagements, that must be the result of a conspiracy, not of individual perversity. He believed that British money was corrupting the federal government, in preparation for restoring a monarchy. Madison could not directly criticize the sainted Washington as an enemy of his country; so he must be considered a mere dupe of the conspiracy, someone not bright enough to see how Hamilton was manipulating him for the benefit of what he and Jefferson called "the anglomen," with their "anglomania." Madison was saying now what Anti-Federalists had said when they opposed his draft of the Constitution—that an evil plan was being advanced under cover of Washington's "great name." Jefferson felt an old saying might apply to him, "Curse on his virtues, they have undone his country" (16.281). He was another Samson shorn of his strength by the seductress Salome/Hamilton (RL 972).

Madison came to see in Hamilton a foe who was destroying his own most fundamental insights into government. Madison had, after all, argued that the federal government of an extended territory would escape narrow interests, yet he now thought Washington's administration was captive to one set of interests. Madison, who had begun the administration as Washington's éminence grise, was now replaced by Hamilton, who administered defeat after defeat to positions taken by Madison and Jefferson. A modern historian sympathetic to Madison says that one result of this development was that Madison became jealous of the man who had replaced him, considering him a kind of usurper.[4] This jealousy would harden into fear and hatred, and would lead to the reversals in Madison's basic positions during the 1790s and, beyond that, to his personal conception of the reasons for the War of 1812.

Only their apocalyptic view of Hamilton's influence can explain the drastic measures Madison and Jefferson took to counter it. They were losing in open arguments with Hamilton's ideas—Jefferson in cabinet discussions with Washington, Madison in votes on the House floor. So they resorted to the covert formation of organized opposition to him, something Madison had hitherto condemned as a deliberate embrace of "factionalism." Nor was Madison alone in the condemnation of faction:

Any public man of probity and conscience in the America of the 1790s who engaged in factional politics would have had to persuade himself, not to say others, that what he was doing in practice did not controvert a theoretical view to which everyone, himself included, subscribed.[5]

The new partisans justified their act in their own minds as a temporary reaction to an extreme crisis. Hamilton's actions amounted to a secret coup, taking over the government. The only way to undermine this undermining was by a secret counterinsurgency. The two men opened this campaign in May 1791 with an exploratory tour of the North, seeking allies under cover of a botany expedition. At the beginning of this tour, they invited Madison's Princeton friend Philip Freneau to breakfast with them in New York, where they asked him to come to Philadelphia and set up an opposition newspaper. Freneau refused, but Madison kept up his efforts to persuade him over the next two months—much as he had maintained his campaign to persuade Washington to go to Philadelphia on the different mission of attending the Constitutional Convention. Jefferson met Freneau's economic worries by giving him a government salary as a State Department translator (J 20.756). Government money would be spent to undermine government policies.

After Freneau gave in and founded the *National Gazette*, Madison contributed to it (anonymously) a series of eleven articles increasingly critical of Washington's administration. His concern to keep this operation secret is clear from his panic when he thought his cover had been blown. Fearing the loss of a *Gazette* manuscript in his own hand, he wrote: "The possibility of its falling into base [i.e., pro-Hamilton] hands cannot be too carefully guarded against. I beg you [Jefferson] to let me know its fate the moment it is in your power" (14.392). What he and Jefferson had initiated soon took on a dynamic of its own. Freneau was hired to attack Hamilton, not Washington (a counterproductive effort if there ever was one). But in shady endeavors of this sort honor can never be presumed. Freneau was soon savaging Washington, and there was nothing Madison and Jefferson could do to restrain him—that would have involved admitting their responsibility for him. Jefferson thought Freneau's journal had veered so out of control that he claimed it was being fooled into articles planted by Federalists to make it look outrageous (J 26.522–23)—though the article that prompted this claim was probably written by Freneau himself.[6] Cat's-paws often end up carrying the cat where it did not want to go.

Actually, defensiveness about Freneau's excesses made his principals feel that, even if he erred, it was in reaction to a provocation that almost justified him. The peril had to be continually ratcheted up to justify the response that had been made to it. So it is that Madison and Jefferson ended up thinking the Washington administration a disaster, held hostage to those who were undoing the Revolution. Jefferson resigned from it in disgust. Madison tried to undermine it. The consensus of historians now is that Washington is among the three greatest presidents of all time (the order differing within the three). But Madison was blind to the extraordinary achievements of Washington. By the end, those achievements could barely be seen, so immense had become the fearsome shadow of Hamilton overarching them in his mind. Jefferson was driven, in his fury at Hamilton, to even wilder covert actions. He secretly drafted a resolution for Senator Giles of Virginia to present in Congress:

Resolved. That the Secretary of the Treasury has been guilty of maladministration in the duties of his office, and should, in the opinion of Congress, be removed from his office by the President of the United States.[7]

To his frustration, this effort, like the other counterinsurgent initiatives, failed—which just contributed to Jefferson's and Madison's obsession with Hamilton.

It is interesting that Hamilton was not similarly obsessed with them. Of course, he did not need to be, since his policies were prevailing in Congress. It is true that he fought Madison's anonymous essays for Freneau with his own anonymous essays in John Fenno's rival paper. But the aggressor had been Madison, and Hamilton, after all, was defending the administration he belonged to, not attacking it. In his dealings with Washington, Hamilton did not question Jefferson's very loyalty to the country, as Jefferson did his. He did not think the two men were fundamentally dishonorable, or enemies to their country. That is why he could recommend Madison as an emissary to France in 1797, and worked actively for Jefferson as president over Aaron Burr in 1800.[8] He thought Jefferson vain, but not corrupt; he considered Madison provincial, but not evil. Anticonspiratorialists cannot afford to entertain such distinctions.

The partisanship that was launched as a temporary response to crisis was soon indurated in the federal city's political life. Congressional delegates had originally clustered in boardinghouses according to the states they came from. By the end of Washington's term and the beginning of Adams's, they roomed with ideological mates. There were Republican boardinghouses and Federalist boardinghouses.[9] The rapid growth of partisanship had been the leading factor in Washington's decision to stay on for a second term, trying to heal this growing wound. If Jefferson and Madison were frustrated at Washington's inability to recognize Hamilton's perfidy, the president was puzzled by their fervid accusations that Hamilton was more loyal to England than to his own country. Washington, after all, had fought side by side with Hamilton against the British. Hamilton was a war hero, the first over the enemy ramparts at Yorktown. Washington, though he did not like to recur to his war memories, would have been less than human if he did not remember, at least fleetingly, how Hamilton had rushed toward the foe at Yorktown while Jefferson had scurried away from him at Monticello.

PRESIDENT ADAMS (1797-1801)

At the end of Washington's second term, Madison was in the government, and Jefferson out. That situation was reversed under the second president. Now Jefferson was back in the government (vice president, since he had come in second to Adams in the electoral college), and Madison was out—he did not run for re-election to the Congress. He had been married for six years at this point, his father was growing old—it was time to take on responsibility for the family plantation, to which Madison gave the name Montpelier in this period. But even in his retirement he watched with concern as President Adams seemed to be submitting to Hamilton's direction, just as Washington had (though Hamilton was out of the government too, practicing law in New York). Madison and Jefferson thought that Adams was searching for an excuse to go to war with France, that he exaggerated the insult given to our ministers there ("the X, Y, Z affair"), and that our navy was being provocative. In what became known as the Quasi-War with France, Congress passed laws that were unconstitutional, forbidding seditious libel and expelling "undesirable aliens." Jefferson withdrew from the Senate, over which he was presiding as vice president while these laws were passed, and returned to Virginia to hatch a plan for nullifying the acts. He went straight to Montpelier to recruit Madison for the effort.

Their earlier attempt to nullify the Jay Treaty, using the amendment process and the fiscal power of the House, had not worked. Obviously, something more drastic was called for in order to nullify these validly passed laws. Jefferson decided to issue a call for the state legislatures to nullify the Alien and Sedition Acts. He would write at least one of these calls, but his part in the operation had to be kept a deep secret. He was, after all, a vice president secretly trying to defeat the regime he belonged to. He would also be a target of the laws he was attacking if his actions were discovered. Despite the risk, however, Jefferson was increasingly coming to rely on the device of planting resolutions in legislatures without revealing that he was their author. He had first tried this with his resolution making Congress call for Hamilton's dismissal from office. Then, in the Adams administration, he drew up a rebuke to a Federalist judge that he maneuvered the Virginia Assembly into presenting as its own (J 17.33–37).

So now he asked Madison to write a call for rescinding the Alien and Sedition Acts, a call to be released by the Virginia Assembly (to which Madison did not belong), while Jefferson would use other agents to release a call from another state, creating the sense of a groundswell of opposition at the state level. At first, Jefferson planned to use North Carolina for this purpose; but a friend from Kentucky said he could get it passed there without betraying its authorship. Jefferson's Kentucky Resolutions said that the offensive laws, "unless arrested at the threshold, necessarily drive these states into revolution and blood."[10] Madison thought this rhetoric inflammatory and tried to get the words for nullification withdrawn. In his own Virginia Resolutions, he said merely that the states should "interpose" to change the laws—a vague word he left for clarification by the states responding to his call. Unfortunately for him, no states (other than Kentucky) did respond. This attempt at nullification was as unsuccessful as the campaign against the Jay Treaty.

From our own historical vantage, we can deplore the Alien and Sedition Acts while realizing that worse excesses have occurred as the result of war scares. The Palmer Raids under Woodrow Wilson arrested thousands and deported over six hundred. The Japanese-American internments under Franklin Roosevelt deprived thousands of their property and liberty. These things occurred without being caused by conspiracies to remake America into a monarchy. But Jefferson and Madison had only one explanation for every governmental evil. Their nullification effort, if others had picked it up, would have been a greater threat to freedom than the misguided laws, which were soon rendered feckless by ridicule and electoral pressure. James Morton Smith, who wrote the classic condemnation of the Alien and Sedition Acts, *Freedom's Fetters*, later wrote of Jefferson's Kentucky Resolutions:

This sweeping claim in the name of states' rights, had it been implemented, would have placed Kentucky in open defiance of federal law; it was an extreme argument that was potentially as dangerous to the Union as the oppressive laws were to individual liberty. (RL 2.1070)

PRESIDENT JEFFERSON (1801-1809)

If Jefferson's role in the Kentucky Resolution had been known, he would probably not have been elected president in 1800. As it was, he won only by the margin given his southern supporters by the inclusion of three-fifths of the slave population in the weighting of electoral votes (an indirect result of Madison's proposal of the three-fifths rule under the Articles). But Jefferson took this slim victory as the second revolution, a restoration from the counter-revolutionary and proto-monarchical administrations that had preceded it. Since those regimes harbored evil, the new one would be all virtue. What Jefferson had called Adams's "reign of the witches" had ended, as he predicted.[11] It has become commonplace in our time for a president from a different party than his predecessor's to do everything possible to distinguish himself from what went before. The election of 1800 was the first chance for that tendency to show itself. Jefferson presented himself as the anti-Adams. Some of his changes were minor, like breaking former protocols at state dinners and the reception of ambassadors. Others were important, like denying former support for the black liberator on Santo Domingo, Toussaint l'Ouverture. Jefferson would still be at this game eight years later, when he righteously said that *he* would make no midnight appointments, as Adams had (it was an easy thing for Jefferson to say, since his successor was Madison, who would not take a new tack): "I shall make no new appointments which can be deferred till the fourth of March, thinking it fair to leave to my successor to select the agents of his own administration" (Dec. 27, 1808).

Jefferson also resembled some later presidents in wanting to be his own secretary of state. He wanted someone who would be more loyal to him than he had been to Washington. He would supply the experience—as would his secretary of the Treasury, Albert Gallatin, who not only knew other countries but had been born in one (Switzerland). Gallatin was the realist in this trio. Having tried his own experimental farming in the West, he had seen through the romantic agrarianism of the other two. Though he had opposed Hamilton when he was in Congress, arguing against the national debt, Gallatin knew that, as secretary of the Treasury, he needed

Hamilton's national bank, and other aspects of his program as well. Gallatin tried to check the other two men's enthusiasm for the embargo—which his department had to enforce.

This team worked together well, but with deeper divisions than appeared from the outside—Jefferson the otherworldly, Madison the provincial, and Gallatin the outvoted. Impressive as the pooled talents of "the triad" have been called by some historians, these men were playing in a league above their heads as the nineteenth century began. The superpowers of the day, France and England, were soon locked in the death grip of the Napoleonic wars. The foreign ministers the United States had to deal with—men like Talleyrand in France, Canning and Castlereagh in England, Godoy in Spain— were playing for high stakes in Europe, and the devious Napoleon was manipulating them all. The United States was a marginal player, sometimes no more than a distraction, in this showdown— though Madison thought it was the key to the whole situation. Only the government that allied itself with America, he believed, could hope to prevail. As early as 1793 he had dreamed of solving the world's problems by using American commerce as a weapon of peaceful coercion: "In this attitude of things, what a noble stroke would be an embargo? It would probably do as much good as harm at home, and would force peace on the rest of the world, and perhaps liberty along with it" (16.215). It was a dream he would labor to make real as secretary of state.

The windfall of the Louisiana Purchase midway in Jefferson's first term (Napoleon almost forced the territory on him) made the president too confident that he could play the great powers off against each other on his own timetable. The purchase, perhaps the greatest bargain in history, had a troubling adjunct that Napoleon used for years to jerk America around, as on a chain—the Floridas. West Florida was what Jefferson was originally trying to buy (along with New Orleans), since southern states wanted the port at Mobile. Madison maintained that it was included in the purchase, though France was equivocal about this and Spain (the occupant) denied it. Jefferson felt that a nod from France would let him seize both Floridas from an enervated Spain, and Napoleon seemed at times on the verge of giving that nod. But then he would back away, keeping America off balance. Jefferson was alternately criticized for cowtowing to Napoleon and for alienating him. In either case he was kept waiting upon his whim. He was learning what it meant to be in the big league.

At times Jefferson, exasperated with Napoleon's kittenish play with him, flirted with the idea of alliance with England. Madison regularly warned against this, reminding Jefferson that England was the real and continuing enemy. Madison looked at England and saw only so many thousands of Hamiltons. Why ally oneself with the source of one's own corruption? This was enough to recall Jefferson to his enduring distrust of England, later put in these terms: "Her good faith! The faith of a nation of merchants! The *Punica fides* of modern Carthage! Of the nation who never admitted a chapter of morality into her political code!"[12] He had written in 1785, "Her [England's] hatred is deep-rooted and cordial and nothing is wanting with her but the power to wipe us and the land we live on out of existence" (J 8.512).

Despite this attitude toward England, Madison felt a particular moment of peril in 1805 when he was absent from Washington with his wife, who was being treated by a Philadelphia physician for a tumor. Jefferson wrote him that he was considering an alliance with England. Madison responded that he would be forced to give away too much, committing America to a war with France. It would be far worse than the Jay Treaty had been:

> If she is to be *bound*, we must be *so too*, either to the same thing, that is, to join her in the war or to do what she will accept as equivalent to such an obligation. What can we offer her? A mutual guaranty, unless so shaped as to involve us pretty certainly in her war, would not be satisfactory. To offer commercial regulations, or concessions on points in the law of nations, as a certain payment for aids which might never be received or required, would be a bargain liable to obvious objections of the most serious kind. (RL 1384, emphasis in original)

Instead of an alliance with England, Madison promoted his own favorite scheme of commercial pressure, which would starve England into submission:

The efficacy of an embargo also cannot be doubted. Indeed, if a commercial weapon can be properly shaped for the Executive hand, it is more and more apparent to me that it can force all the nations having colonies in this quarter of the globe to respect our rights. (RL 1285)

This disastrous plan was eventually adopted by Jefferson because it fit so perfectly into his cluster of ideological presuppositions:

A belief in executive forbearance, fiscal predilections that abhorred debt, a faith that standing armies and navies necessarily corroded freedom, a reliance on militia, an adherence to commercial coercion, and a long-range view that America was impregnable were, however correct and virtuous by themselves, dangerous when insisted upon categorically in a world at war. . . . By learning too slowly the exigencies of power, the Republicans endangered national survival. (K 471)

When the French were seizing American ships at sea in the 1790s, President Adams had prepared for war and reached an agreement in the treaty of Morfontaine. Jefferson, the anti-Adams, had deliberately deprived America of a war capacity, since he felt that this would be an invitation to war. Why threaten force when a rational neutrality, backed by commercial deprivation of any who violate the neutrality, could attain the desired object?

So Jefferson proposed a Madisonian embargo. Congress passed the bill. Some legislators thought it was a way of buying time to come up with other measures, meanwhile keeping our ships at home to avoid danger. Some thought it was itself a preparation for war (Gallatin hoped it was). Many did not believe Jefferson meant to maintain it indefinitely (it would go on for fifteen months). Defiance of it began immediately and escalated, as did Jefferson's determination to support it with force. The exports of America were barely a fifth in 1808 of what they had been in 1807. The depression this caused led to outright defiance of the law, which Jefferson grimly mobilized troops to enforce. He called on the regular army, on inspectors, on informers to wage war on smugglers. Leonard Levy, the constitutional historian, notes:

On a prolonged, widespread, and systematic basis, in some places lasting nearly a year, the armed forces harried and beleaguered the citizenry. Never before or since did American history exhibit such a spectacle of derangement of normal values and perspectives. . . . This was the only time in American history that the President was empowered to use the army for routine or day-to-day execution of the laws.[13]

Jefferson, without realizing it, was reverting to the stand young Madison had taken in the Revolution, thinking mere suspicion of disloyalty prima facie proof of it. Concerning citizens of towns where smuggling had occurred, Jefferson wrote: "In such a case we may fairly require positive proof that the individual of a town tainted with a general spirit of disobedience has never said or done anything himself to countenance that spirit."[14] There were so many smugglers liable to execution that Jefferson demanded authority to monitor their prosecutions to achieve maximum public effect: "If all these people are convicted, there will be too many to be punished with death. My hope is that they [the prosecutors] will send me full statements of every man's case, that the most guilty may be marked as examples, and the less suffer long imprisonments, under reprieves from time to time."[15] Jefferson had set up a state terrorism that made the Alien and Sedition prosecutions under Adams look minor by comparison.

Though Gallatin kept saying that the embargo could not be continued without unparalleled state repression, Madison supported it with unflagging confidence. As the effort faltered, he kept saying that it would work if it were just prolonged longer, enforced harder, made more inclusive, and used as a test of republican orthodoxy. In time the British and French outrages at sea would "rivet" the embargo on American purpose, to "reconcile all parties to it" (K 459). Madison gave rosy accounts of the embargo's success to our diplomats abroad—"the public mind everywhere is rallying to the policy," there was "not the slightest indication of a purpose to rescind [it]" (K 459). When Jefferson himself began to harbor doubts, Madison tried to dispel them. Federalists had for a long time called Madison the mere puppet of Jefferson. But Senator William Plumer, seeing deeper, realized that Madison had now become the steering partner: "Madison has acquired a complete ascendancy over him" (K 472).

Jefferson had nowhere else to turn for confidence that he was doing the right thing. Gallatin could not offer support for the deteriorating program. Even when a frustrated Jefferson suspended his executive activity, surrendering the problem to his successor, Madison was still saying that Congress must "make the Embargo proof against the frauds which have evaded it, which can be done with an effect little apprehended abroad" (K 464)—that is, Congress could become even more draconian in punishment, without alerting other nations to the degree of resistance being mounted. But in fact the French and British already knew how unpopular the embargo was at home— they learned this not only from their representatives in America, but from smugglers who succeeded in evading the patrols and took their products abroad. Foreign governments professed satisfaction that the policy was hurting America more than it did them. John Armstrong, United States minister to France, wrote of the embargo, "Here it is not felt, and in England . . . it is forgotten."

Finally, Congress could take no more. Against the urgings of Madison, it voted to end the embargo. As a kind of gratuitous insult to Jefferson, the date of its expiration was set for the day he would be leaving office.

II.

The Presidency:
First Term (1809−1813)

4

Policy and Personnel
(1809)

More, probably, than any other president on first taking office, Madison knew what lay ahead of him. As secretary of state, not only had he spent eight years at Jefferson's elbow. He had for four months been trying to jog that elbow as Jefferson lapsed into a weird torpor through the whole last third of his last year in office. Many attempts have been made to explain this paralysis. Henry Adams thought that losing his popularity was like being cutting off from the very air Jefferson needed to breathe.[1] Leonard White attributed the lethargy to a massive loss of self-confidence.[2] The resolutely admiring Dumas Malone thinks that Jefferson was just tired—though no other president has offered this excuse, and the pace of business was such in the eighteenth century that, even as president, Jefferson spent three months a year at Monticello.[3] Robert Johnstone thought the collapse showed an inability to resolve conflict: "One of the recognized methods among political actors for the resolution of conflict is illness or resignation. One form of 'resignation' might well be a psychological abdication of power."[4] Others think that the man of such infectious optimism was unable to act when he could no longer find an optimistic way of looking at events (something similar seems to have happened, toward the end of his life, when he could no longer foresee a gradual disappearance of slavery). It has also been supposed that he buckled under the strain of using quasi-dictatorial powers to enforce the embargo. The man who had expanded executive power to an unparalleled extent seemed to be horrified at what he was doing, and his hand fell nerveless from the instrument it had framed.[5]

One problem with this last explanation is that Jefferson's abdication was not unique to the embargo situation. He had done this before. In 1781, when he found he could do nothing as governor to cope with the British invasion of Virginia, he called for Washington to bring the Continental army there and take over the reins from him (J 6.33). When Washington, who had a few other states to think of, rejected that desperate plea, and when Jefferson was driven out of his home by the British, he went off to his retreat at Poplar Forest, and did nothing to help transfer power to his successor in the governorship, Thomas Nelson. This strange conduct led to an official investigation to determine if he had been derelict in office (J 6.106–7). In the same way he resigned from Washington's cabinet, leaving it with no strong Republican voice, when he felt that Washington was listening too much to Hamilton—though "Jefferson in fact exaggerated the odds that he faced, for Washington sided with him as often as with Hamilton."[6] Washington sincerely wanted to have a balance of views. Jefferson quotes him as pleading not "to be deserted by those on whom he had counted" (J 26.627–30). A third time, when the sedition law was being passed, he walked away from the Senate, where he had been presiding, to go into internal exile from the administration he belonged to.

But the worst defection occurred when he gave up governing the nation for four crucial months, passing on a stalled executive to his successor, Madison. "So cowed was he as to do what no President had ever done before, or has ever done since, and what no President has a constitutional right to do: he abdicated the duties of his office, and no entreaty could induce him to resume them" (G 377). Jefferson claimed that he was doing this as a favor to Madison: "I have thought it right to take no part myself in proposing measures the execution of which will devolve on my successors. I am therefore chiefly an unmeddling listener to what others say" (G 377). But Madison and Gallatin urged Jefferson to take charge, not to let the nation drift. Gallatin put it in writing: "Both Mr. Madison and myself concur in opinion that, considering the temper of the Legislature, or rather of its members, it would be eligible [desirable] to point out to them some precise and distinct course"

(RL 1557). It was the central pillar of the triad that had crumbled, and the other two could do nothing about it. The paralysis did not go unnoticed by the Federalists. Josiah Quincy wrote to John Adams that they had "a dish of skim-milk at the head of our nation," one whose only thought was "away to Monticello, and let the Devil take the hindmost" (A 1172).

Perhaps the best way to explain what happened to Jefferson is to start from his great gift for seeing large principle and sacred duty in every political decision he made. This is what clothed his every action in such stirring rhetoric. It is also what made him see opponents, not as motivated by personal error or interest, but as acting on principles as large as his but antithetical to them. Those vast conspiracies were symmetrical antitypes to his grand designs of virtue. One problem with that gift is that Jefferson could not maneuver as pragmatically as most politicians are required to do. This did not mean that he was incapable of taking opportunistic steps, as he did in purchasing Louisiana. But at each change of course he had to invent a new set of absolute principles to elucidate it. That is why Jefferson can be so tellingly quoted on so many sides of various issues. Whatever he was doing at the moment had a radiantly eternal rationale. But in 1808 he at last faced a situation where he could find no rationale for any of the choices facing him. There were really only three. 1) Prolong the failed embargo. 2) Submit to British outrages at sea. 3) Resist those outrages by going to war. The first two had become unthinkable. And Jefferson refused to think about the third. Otherworldliness, when unable to cope with the world, just seals the world out. The great theorizing capacity that had energized Jefferson and his followers over the years, finding no space left for its operation, just shorted out, just shut down. The system went dark.

No wonder Madison took office with some qualms. And no wonder he hoped that Jefferson could come up with some program to follow on Congress's repeal of the embargo, because *he* could not. He continued to think that the embargo had been working, it just needed to be carried on for a longer time with more vigorous enforcement. He was like the Americans who believe the Vietnam War was being won, we just gave up on it too early. At the very time when Congress was about to cancel the embargo, Madison was pleading for its "invigoration" (S 24). This was a mysterious matter for him, since he had posed the embargo as a contest between English vice and America virtue. In what he called "a contest of privations" (S 24) the Americans should have been able, and the English unable, to give up the luxuries of trade for the benefits of honor. The failure to do this remained a mystery to him all his life: "No measure was ever adopted by so great a proportion of any public body which found the hearty concurrence of so small a one" (K 491).

We have seen earlier instances of Madison's clinging to a plan so obviously right in his own mind that he cannot recognize its impracticability. But the worst of his obsessions was the embargo. As Orchard Cook wrote to John Quincy Adams, he was "inclined to hug the embargo, and die in its embrace" (RL 1553). It was his feckless yearning back toward the embargo that made him not only inherit but prolong Jefferson's period of drift—what J. C. A. Stagg refers to as "the political paralysis that characterized Madison's first two years in the presidency" (S 52). This stalled start of his presidency is usually attributed to his bad personnel choices, and there is much to criticize in those. But the personnel mistakes followed on the policy fixation. The embargo died on the very day Madison took office, replaced by an ineffectual nonintercourse act, abandoning not all trade, only that with England and France. The new policy was even less enforceable than the embargo, and would have had little effect even if it could have been enforced. Madison saw these flaws in the scheme, but had nothing to improve it, nothing to propose but a recurrence to the embargo.

The obvious next step, after the demise of the embargo, was to prepare for war. Even if Madison had no real intent to go to war, preparation for it would give force to whatever other policies could be found, both at home and abroad. It would be another form of the "contest of privation" that Madison considered an exercise of virtue. But Madison, like Jefferson, had an ideological block about war of any kind. This was not because of any distaste for killing. (Slaveholders were not in general squeamish.) Though Jefferson jokingly referred to his "quaker" policy, his real objection was that war entails debt and taxes, the Federalist sins that corrupt a nation. As Madison put it in his "Political Observations" of 1795, "War is the parent of armies; from these proceed debts and taxes; and armies, and debts, and taxes are the known instruments for bringing the many under the domination of the few."[7] Jefferson, just two weeks after he left office, wrote a letter urging Madison to keep the faith on the subject of war. The "lying and licentious" press was misleading Congress, which would do great damage in the protracted sessions necessitated by a war. Even normal considerations of national honor should be suspended during the Napoleonic conflagration in Europe. "Nor in the present maniac state of Europe should I estimate the point of honor by the ordinary scale. I believe we shall on the contrary have credit with the world for having made the avoidance of being engaged in the present unexampled war our first object" (RL 1576).

Madison's staffing of his administration showed that he was denying himself even the possibility of considering war. He appointed Republicans as secretaries of war and navy, but that was their only qualification other than geographical spread—William Eustis for war came from Massachusetts, Paul Hamilton for navy from South Carolina. Eustis was a physician whose sole military experience had come as a hospital surgeon in the Revolution. Hamilton had been an undistinguished governor of his state ten years ago—he was also an alcoholic who could do little productive work after his noon imbibings (B 5.126). Did Madison know that when he appointed him? It was his business to know it. In any event, he knew soon after, and yet kept him on. Foreign ministers in Washington needed nothing more than a glance at these men to inform their governments that Madison offered them no threat of war. The men were as fit for their posts as Benjamin Franklin would have been for the corps de ballet.

There was only one man Madison *must* have in his cabinet, and he was not permitted to put him where he wanted him, as his own replacement at the State Department. Albert Gallatin had enemies in Pennsylvania, headed by the family of Senator Samuel Smith, who could call on a network of powerful connections in the Republican party, including Wilson Cary Nicholas in the Virginia legislature and the violently anti-Gallatin newspaper, the Philadelphia *Aurora*. "The Smith and Nicholas families were united by three marriages, and their friends and relatives were politically influential in New York, Maryland, and Virginia" (S 61). Senator William

Branch Giles of Virginia, marshaling these dissident Republicans, wanted to become secretary of state himself (Jefferson and Madison had gone on from that post to the presidency). Giles presented Madison with an ultimatum, listing nine reasons why the Senate would never confirm Gallatin as secretary of state (R 16–17).

Several of these reasons glanced at Gallatin's involvement with the policies of Jefferson and Madison. Thus for Madison to abandon Gallatin would be to abandon his own political record. It would make him a captive of the Senate Republicans who were backing Giles. Instead of taking on this group at the outset, he hoped to wear them down with long-term negotiation—his old legislative strategy, out of keeping with his present executive post. He struck a halfway bargain by keeping Gallatin at Treasury, where he would not need another Senate confirmation, and keeping Giles out of the Department of State post by bringing in Samuel Smith's brother, Robert. This could be considered a neat ploy in terms of the backstage maneuvers Madison used in committees and conventions. But Smith was in a sneaky way almost as bad as Giles would have been in his confrontational way. That Robert Smith had been an incompetent secretary of navy under Jefferson had not mattered much, since Jefferson, who wanted to do without a navy, had no objection to letting a nullity preside over a vacuity. But his presence in the most important cabinet office meant that Madison could not rely on Smith's reports from foreign representatives, and that Madison himself would have to compose any foreign dispatches where precision was important. Smith's disloyalty meant that he was always conspiring with his faction to undermine Gallatin in the cabinet. He had battled Gallatin when he was secretary of the navy, since Gallatin resolutely cut the navy's budget. This battle bound the Maryland Smiths to the "Old Democrats" of Pennsylvania who had a long-standing feud with Gallatin.

Madison began with one disloyal member of his administration, about whom he could do nothing. George Clinton, a leader of New York Republicans opposed to Madison, let his name stand in 1808 for the presidency *and* for vice president on Madison's ticket. He thus became a critic within the administration, a vice president presiding over the Senate in case of tie votes and deciding issue against Madison. Having Smith in the cabinet as well meant that Madison experienced the kind of disloyalty Jefferson had shown to Washington as his secretary of state (funding Freneau to attack the government) and had shown to Adams as his vice president (drafting state resolutions against the government). Madison's cabinet proved less an instrument for him to use than a problem for him to struggle with:

> Madison was often at odds with at least one of his colleagues—who were also at odds with each other—and he had developed as a consequence the habit of tolerating, usually by recourse to ambiguity, personal differences of opinion rather than trying to settle them. . . . Consequently, the President dealt with many serious problems only when he could no longer avoid the difficulties his own methods had created. (S 506)

Madison called fewer cabinet meetings than had his predecessors. He tended to consult the secretaries in their own offices (R 33). This harked back to his practice, in Congress, of consulting members privately. But since these consultations replaced expectable cabinet meetings, they provided Smith with a new grievance, as he realized that Gallatin was being consulted more often, even on foreign policy, than was the secretary of state. This was a situation that could only deteriorate, until Gallatin at length forced a resolution on Madison by making it clear that he must choose—either Smith must go or he would. Smith went, but only after two years had been wasted trying to work an unworkable arrangement. And by then Smith had accumulated information for embarrassing those who drove him out.

Perhaps Madison's worst decision on personnel did not concern the cabinet, or any political offices in Washington. It had to do with a military general, James Wilkinson. Madison's decision to retain Wilkinson in his position was the result of scrutiny protracted through most of his first term, and it came back to haunt him during the war in his second term. Wilkinson was appointed in the waning months of Jefferson's administration to take charge of new troops being raised to protect New Orleans from any foreign interference. Wilkinson, knowing that Jefferson aspired to annex Cuba to the United States, traveled to New Orleans by way of Havana, to see what exploitable opportunities it might offer to his scheming disposition.

When he finally arrived at New Orleans, early in Madison's term, he took charge of troops who were suffering extraordinary casualties from disease. Madison's secretary of war, William Eustis, had only one qualification for his office, his service at camp hospitals in the Revolution. He noticed the statistics on disease in New Orleans, and ordered Wilkinson to move the troops to higher and drier ground, away from the malarial swamps. Wilkinson disregarded the order, later maintaining that the men were too sick to move. He left them in swampy lowlands until, when they were belatedly moved, as many died in that effort as had perished in the swamps. He lost half of the 2,000 men committed to his care—816 to death, the rest to desertion (R 58).

Wilkinson, who had a magic of shamelessness that carried him through scandal after scandal, went on the offensive after a preliminary investigation found him responsible for the deaths of his men. He knew he was the object of Jefferson's protection, since he had turned state's evidence against Aaron Burr, with whom he had been engaged in possibly treasonous plotting. Jefferson in his second term had become almost as obsessed with Burr as he had earlier been with Hamilton; and when another of his foes, Justice John Marshall, presided over the trial that freed Burr, Jefferson retained the services of the badly tainted Wilkinson, to keep him loyal to the last of his many stories about Burr's activities. Wilkinson now called on that commitment, and on other Republicans who had compromising ties with him—Robert Smith had brought into the State Department John Colvin, who ghostwrote Wilkinson's memoirs (B 5.131). Jefferson wrote Madison a new character reference (RL 1664–65). Madison, thus put on the spot, hoped that a full court-martial would find Wilkinson guilty and take him off the president's hands.

When the military tribunal waffled, and Madison had to dispose of the matter personally, he agonized over it, studying all the tribunal's proceedings. Then he exonerated Wilkinson. One can imagine the quick work George Washington would have made of a general who willfully destroyed a thousand of his own troops. Madison's weak response to this problem retained a man in command who would be responsible for more needless deaths in the

War of 1812. Madison's decision is roundly condemned in Robert Rutland's study of his presidency:

Madison's handling of the Wilkinson case was damaging to his presidency and was probably the worst mistake he made while in the White House. Not only did he saddle the country with an incompetent soldier, he also kept alive the whitewash started by Jefferson with a military decision made for political reasons. Once Wilkinson was permitted to keep his command, he was an albatross the Republican presidents thought they had to protect. This was a bad precedent, leading to further politicalization of the army and navy, with disastrous consequence that would keep cropping up during the Mexican War and would get completely out of hand during the Civil War, when commands were dispensed not for ability but to safeguard party control of the White House. Some of this would undoubtedly have happened even if Madison had done the right thing and sacked Wilkinson when he had the chance. But by dodging his responsibility, Madison harmed the war effort, hurt the army's morale, and in effect became a buck-passer instead of a courageous leader. (R 59)[8]

Once again policy contributed to a bad personnel decision—Madison's early policy of refusing to treat war as a real possibility, whose outcome could depend on the retention of an unreliable military officer.

5

Domestic Affairs: The Partisans
(1809–1816)

When Madison and Jefferson set up their partisan opposition to
Washington's "Hamiltonian" policies, it was as a counterinsurgency
to block a coup. The response to the crisis was supposed to cease
with the crisis. That is what Jefferson meant when he said in his
1801 inaugural address that the ideological war was over: "We are
all Republicans, we are all Federalists." But he found that the war
was not so easily called off. What about the Federalists, appointed
by President Adams, who were still in government? The appointments to the judiciary could not be dismissed, though repeal of the
Adams judiciary act would cut back their scope. Non-judicial "midnight appointments" could be and were dismissed. But beyond that
Jefferson's proclaimed ideal was to retain or add officials only on
the basis of merit, not party—which meant that Federalist appointments should be dismissed only for malfeasance or incompetence.

But Jefferson's own allies were not satisfied with this. The editor
of the Republican paper *Aurora* in Philadelphia called for a clean
sweep of Federalists from all appointments. Jefferson said that a
balance of fifty-fifty might be struck as a temporary step toward the
merit-only policy, which could be fully implemented when, as he
predicted, the parties disappeared during his term of office. But
when Albert Gallatin, whose office of the Treasury had a large
patronage in customs officials at the ports, drew up a circular saying

that "integrity and capacity" would be the only criteria for employment, Jefferson ordered him not to issue it, since he could not "absolutely revolt our tried friends" (G 279–81). Gallatin's policy was known and resented, however, especially by Republicans in his own state of Pennsylvania. The effects of that disagreement would still be haunting Madison, eight years later, when he found Pennsylvania Republicans in the faction opposed to making Gallatin secretary of state.

Partisanship was not something that faded after 1800, not even after the drastic fall of Federalist influence during Jefferson's first term. The Republicans split into factions, which soon became more difficult to handle than the Federalists had been. There were at least four nuclei of dissent, sometimes in league with each other, sometimes at daggers drawn.

1. The "Old Republicans" were agrarian purists, strict constructionists like John Randolph of Roanoke and John Taylor of Caroline, states rightists who thought that Jefferson and Madison were betraying "true Republicanism" by extending federal power. They opposed military preparation and the navy. Monroe had been allied with them when he was their candidate against Madison. Their party was an "odd third" (tertium quid) added to the two-party conflict of Federalists with regular Republicans, so they were called "quids."

2. The Clintonites of New York were an original part of the Republican coalition that united North and South, but had problems with the embargo and felt that they were not given their share of patronage. The followers of the Revolutionary governor George Clinton and his nephew DeWitt Clinton wanted to break the Virginia hold on the presidency by advancing one or other of the Clintons to that office.

3. The "Invisibles," so called for their backstage maneuvers, largely coordinated in the Senate by members from Pennsylvania (Michael Leib), Maryland (Samuel Smith), and Virginia (William Branch Giles). Their voice was William Duane, the frothing Anglophobe editor of the Philadelphia *Aurora*.

4. The regular Republicans, loyal supporters of the Jefferson administration, were nibbled at or propped up by these competing factions during Madison's presidency. He had no majority without one or two of these dissident groups (according to the issue), but he did not settle on wooing just one or two. His temperament and experience made him omnidirectionally deferential. We saw in the last chapter how that worked in the nomination of Robert Smith for secretary of state. Madison could not choose between Gallatin the regular and Smith the "Invisible," so his cabinet became a cockpit of rivalries. He had a Clintonite (George Clinton himself) for vice president, whose followers he tried to placate, while making an unsuccessful overture to the old Republicans by offering a government post to Monroe (turned down as not important enough). It was difficult to build support for his policies, at home or abroad, out of these friable elements. This became apparent with matters like Supreme Court appointments, Yazoo land, the Bank of the United States, and the Floridas.

THE COURT

Jefferson had been unable to break the Federalist stronghold on the Supreme Court, since he had no opportunity to replace a justice. When William Cushing died at age seventy-eight on September 13, 1810, Jefferson rejoiced to Madison that this was a "godsend." But party considerations made it impossible for Madison to fill that post for over a year, by which time another seat on the bench had come open. At last he had to fall back on a replacement for Cushing who joined with the Federalist majority on the Court, dissipating the opportunity Jefferson had seen.

Since Cushing was a New Englander, and Supreme Court justices of that day rode circuit in their districts, the replacement had to come from New England. It was hard for Madison to find a Republican of established legal experience in what had until recently been a Federalist stronghold. It was also hard to find a Republican who had backed the embargo, since that Jeffersonian disaster had been most energetically resisted in the merchant North. What was wanted was a non-dissident Republican, one who was also from New England, and Madison agreed with Jefferson that former attorney general

Levi Lincoln of Massachusetts met these requirements. Though Jefferson had promised to appoint for merit, not for partisan reasons, he recommended putting a man on the Supreme Court who had little to recommend him but partisan alignment. Jefferson wrote Madison of their favored candidate, Lincoln:

> I know you think lightly of him as a lawyer; and I do not consider him as a correct common lawyer, yet as much so as anyone which ever came, or ever can come, from one of the eastern [New England] states. Their system of jurisprudence, made up from the Jewish [puritanical] law, a little dash of common law, etc., a great mass of original notions of their own, is a thing *sui generis*, and one educated in that system can never so far eradicate early impressions as to imbibe thoroughly the principles of another system. (P 2.581)

The seat was offered to Lincoln, but he was going blind in 1810 and declined the nomination. He recommended Barnabas Bidwell, the attorney general of Massachusetts; but before Madison could approach Bidwell, the man disappeared over the Canadian border, fleeing charges of financial irregularities in his office. Republicans in New England then proposed Madison's own postmaster general, Gideon Granger, who campaigned actively for the job, reminding Madison that he had defended Dolley Madison from detractors and reminding Jefferson that he had attacked rumors of his love affair with a friend's wife. Mention of these embarrassments as a basis for appointment made Madison call Granger's self-promotion self-defeating (P 3.57). After Granger was passed over, he took his revenge in 1814 by giving the Pennsylvania postmaster post to Madison's bitter critic, Michael Leib, who resigned from the Senate to take the lucrative job. This was too much even for the exceedingly patient Madison. He fired Granger, who then made vague threats of blackmail to Jefferson by promising revelations from the Burr prosecution (RL 1740).

Madison continued his search for a New Englander who had supported Jeffersonian Republicans (including the embargo), but he had almost exhausted that rare breed. One specimen, Alexander Wolcott, met the criteria all too well—he had organized the Republican Party in Connecticut and been a ferocious pamphleteer for the whole Jeffersonian program, creating friction by his demands for ideological discipline. The Senate, unhappy that Madison made his first Supreme Court nomination so blatantly partisan, rejected Wolcott by a resounding vote (twenty-four to nine). Irving Brant, normally well disposed toward Madison, wrote: "To nominate so well-hated a man for the Supreme Court, with no testimonial to his judicial fitness, was a first-rate political blunder" (B 5.170).

Madison tried to recover by offering the post to John Quincy Adams. He was a Federalist, but he had gone against his party to support the embargo, and been rewarded with appointment as minister to Russia. The Senate quickly confirmed Adams, even before he had a chance to respond from Saint Petersburg. The response, when it did come, was a refusal—Adams had his eye on a higher office, the one he achieved in 1824. By this point, the Senate had rejected the man who was willing to serve and accepted the man who was unwilling. Madison held off on further nomination until the fall of 1811, hoping that new elections would change the complexion of the Senate sufficiently for him to get a Republican who had supported the embargo confirmed. (Jefferson, in his communications with the president, had made this a litmus test.) When no serious changes were made in the Senate, Madison was driven back on a choice that Jefferson had privately denounced, the young (thirty-two-year-old) legal star from Massachusetts, Joseph Story. Story was a Republican, but he had voted against the embargo, and he confirmed on the bench Jefferson's fears of his "Tory" inclinations. But at least Madison could get him confirmed.

The partisan calculus over the second seat to be filled was simpler. Samuel Chase, the justice whom Jeffersonians had impeached but failed to convict in 1805, finally died on June 19, 1811. Since Chase came from Pennsylvania, the Senate problem to be solved was picking a man satisfactory to the Pennsylvania Invisibles. Luckily for Madison, there was such a man in his own administration, one he got along with himself and who had family friendships with Michael Leib—Comptroller of the Treasury Gabriel Duvall. Though Duvall had little other distinction, Madison was relieved to get at least one non-controversial man confirmed, a year after the Cushing vacancy had opened up. The whole nominating process had suggested presidential weakness, and had not changed the course of the Court at all.

YAZOO CHARGES

One reason Madison wanted to alter the makeup of the Supreme Court was its decision, *Fletcher v. Peck*, on April 16, 1810. John Marshall, writing for the Court, overthrew a settlement that Madison had brokered when he was secretary of state. This involved the Yazoo land scandal of 1795, when a corrupt Georgia legislature had taken bribes to peddle fraudulent claims to millions of acres of land in its western territory (some of the claims already sold or granted the Indians by treaties). When a reform legislature was elected in 1796, it voided the claims that had been invalidly sold. The holders of the false claims, however, many of whom came from the North, argued that they had made their purchases in good faith and deserved either recognition of the claims or recompense for their loss. The state of Georgia refused to surrender its western territory to these speculators, or to pay them for settling it. Constitutional and practical obstacles were raised by individuals or corporations from other states trying to sue a state legislature.

Jefferson, on becoming president in 1801, inherited this conflict, which was dividing northern and southern parts of his new Republican coalition. He appointed a committee, made up of his secretary of state (Madison), secretary of the Treasury (Gallatin), and attorney general (Levi Lincoln), to investigate the issues and recommend a bill to Congress for settling the controversy. The committee would be accused of conflicts of interest, since Madison and Gallatin each had a brother-in-law who supported the claimants (B 4.237), and Jefferson's postmaster general, Gideon Granger, one of the chief claimants, had given patronage posts to supporters of the claims.

The compromise worked out by Jefferson's committee contained the following elements—Georgia's cession of the disputed territory to the United States in return for a million and a quarter of federal money, the formation of new states from the territory, the invalidation of all but four land companies' claims, the sequestration of five million acres of unclaimed land to be divided between the remaining four companies with valid claims, or to be sold, with the proceeds going proportionally to the claimants. Like any good compromise, this one let no single party get everything it wanted. Georgia had to give up its land, the claimants lost all or part of their property, the defenders of strict construction lost their ban on federal acquisition of territory, the defenders of states' rights lost their immunity from federal overrides of state law.

As can readily be seen, the committee recommendations were full of potential embarrassments for a Republican administration, a point John Randolph and others were ready to rub in. When it was Virginia's land (not Georgia's) that was being ceded, Madison (then in the Continental Congress) had fought the claims of northern land speculators—but now he was defending them. He had proposed in the Constitutional Convention that the federal government should veto state laws, while in the interval he had composed the Virginia Resolutions to resist such "usurpation"—and now he was overriding the state law that invalidated northern claims. At the very time when the committee was investigating the Georgia transaction, Jefferson was harboring constitutional doubts about his ability to acquire the Louisiana Territory from a willing foreigner (Napoleon)—but here was his committee trying to acquire territory to be taken away from an unwilling United States party (the state of Georgia).

Given these entanglements, it is not surprising that the congressional enactment needed to legitimate and finance the complex arrangement was denied the committee in 1805, leaving the whole matter unresolved, with claims still being litigated in various courts. That is the situation the Supreme Court addressed in the second year of Madison's presidency. It denied both the earlier attempts at settlement and upheld the rights of the claimants. John Marshall's opinion said that Georgia could not void its contracts and that the federal committee could not impose a partial rescission of those contracts. This guaranteed that the Yazoo issue would continue to plague Madison throughout most of his presidency. John Randolph had denounced him as a "Yazoo man" when the compromise was presented to Congress in Jefferson's first term. The Philadelphia *Aurora* renewed those charges of corruption when Madison ran for his first term in 1808 (B 4.434).

The Yazoo issue came up with many of his nominations. Levi Lincoln, whom he wanted to put on the Court, had been part of the Yazoo committee—as had Gallatin, whom he wanted to make secretary of state. Another of his nominations for the Court was John Quincy Adams, who had served as counsel to the claimants in *Fletcher.* So had Joseph Story, the nominee after Adams. Gideon Granger, his postmaster general, was one of the wealthy claimants to Yazoo land, and it was said that his patronage for postmasterships favored other claimants or the supporters of their suit. The attacks on a venal cabal of speculators that Madison had leveled against Hamilton and his allies were now turned on him by Randolph and the other critics of his administration. Even Madison's attempts to seize West Florida from Spain were said to be prompted by Yazoo interests, since the Georgia claims ran along and into the borders of West Florida. The partisan attacks on "Yazoo men" were not blunted until the middle of Madison's second term, when Congress appropriated over four million dollars to pay off the claimants. This, plus the amounts paid to Georgia and to Indians whose treaties were bought off, made the total costs of the Yazoo lands exceed the fifteen million dollars paid for the whole Louisiana Territory.[1]

THE BANK

The charter for the Bank of the United States was scheduled to lapse in March of 1811. This was, of course, the institution that Jefferson and Madison had denounced as unconstitutional, during Washington's presidency, when Hamilton won the battle to found it. Jefferson had continued his hostility into the nineteenth century, and added partisan motives to his view of its unconstitutionality. In his own first term as president, Jefferson wrote to Gallatin, his secretary of the Treasury:

> I am decidedly in favor of making all the [local] banks Republican by sharing deposits among them in proportion to the dispositions they show. If the law now forbids it, we should not permit another session of Congress to pass without

amending it. It is material to the safety of Republicanism to detach the mercantile interest from its enemies and incorporate them into the body of its friends. (G 309)

This was written three years after Jefferson had announced the death of partisanship, saying, "We are all Republicans, we are all Federalists."

By 1811, Madison had changed his mind on the bank, though he did not want to make an open break with Jefferson on the issue. He privately assured people that his arguments against the bank, though sound at the time, had been rendered inapplicable by long usage (unconstitutional things become constitutional if they are accepted as such?). Gallatin was now an energetic promoter of the bank. Jefferson's embargo had slashed the Treasury's principal source of income, customs duties, and he needed loans that no other source would give on the terms available from the bank. The Republican party, born out of a hatred for the financial credit system, now depended on it for its survival. Gallatin pleaded with Congress to renew the charter—but he got no public support from his president. He needed support, since Gallatin's enemies in the Senate took his advocacy as a proof of his own corruption, turning against him the charges Madison had leveled at Hamilton.

Congressional forces from the new states in the West, led by Kentucky's Henry Clay, had the populist instinct for easy credit that made them distrust eastern sound-money men. These men took up Madison's original assaults on the bank, which had been reprinted and circulated. It was widely assumed that he had changed his mind—Gallatin would not take a position at odds with his president's. But the grounds for his change, if any, were unknown. Nathaniel Macon, an important congressional chairman, complained: "When great men, or rather men in high responsible station, change their deliberate opinions, it seems to me that they in some way or other ought to give the reason for the change" (G 427).

The struggle was so close that Madison's active campaigning for the bank would have saved it. Instead, he hoped to influence the course of the debate by the backstage tactics of his legislative days. The result was a tie vote in the Senate, which was broken by his own vice president, George Clinton, sealing the bank's fate with a vote against the administration. What explains Madison's unwillingness to enter the fray? Partly, no doubt, he did not want to have an open break with Jefferson. But his admiring biographer, Irving Brant, claims that he was spooked by the reprinting of his old arguments, triggering "Madison's lifelong unwillingness to make a public display of political inconsistency."

Having found the bank to be a useful adjunct to the Treasury, he was ready to let it be known quietly that he regarded its unchallenged existence for twenty years as evidence of its constitutionality. If he had taken that stand in a message to Congress, his own party would have produced the few votes needed to pass the measure in both houses. (B 5.269–70)

This judgment might be a considered too harsh if there were not ample later evidence of Madison's desire to cover over inconsistencies in his record.

The troubles Gallatin predicted if the bank were abolished came true in the War of 1812, when funds to wage it had to be sought from taxes and from reluctant lenders at ruinous rates—both of them sources that Republicans abominated. In Madison's seventh annual message to Congress, in 1815, he would say that "the benefits of an uniform national currency should be restored to the community . . . the probable operation of a national bank will merit consideration."[2] This closed the costly circular motion away from and back to a bank that was never more needed than when it was absent. Congress passed the new charter and Madison signed it into law, with nary a croak about its constitutionality. Henry Clay, the great excoriater of the bank in 1811, came down from the speaker's chair in the House to champion its re-adoption in 1814. By now it had become essential to his internal improvement plans for the West. After he retired from Congress, he became legal counsel to the Second Bank of the United States.

THE FLORIDAS

Though Madison's recurrent quest to acquire the Floridas was a matter of international diplomacy, the process was inextricably woven into domestic disputes, both sectional and ideological. The original aim of Jefferson had been to acquire West Florida along with New Orleans, since the southern states wanted to move their produce through the port at Mobile. (West Florida then included the margins of the Gulf of Mexico that now belong to Mississippi and Alabama.) James Monroe, negotiating that purchase, was offered the whole Louisiana territory—which, he claimed, included West Florida, since France had owned the two regions together before Spain did. Spain's retrocession of Louisiana must therefore, according to Monroe's shaky logic, have been a retrocession of West Florida as well. Madison, as secretary of state, defended Monroe's claim, though Spain denied it and France equivocated. The Jefferson administration decided to maintain a legal right to the property, but not to act on it until Spain was in no condition to resist. Practically, that meant until France gave the United States a signal to seize the prize. Madison said that Florida was like a ripe pear that would drop in its own time. But it proved a Tantalus pear, forever being whisked away just when it seemed ready to drop.

Since Spain maintained only a thin military presence in West Florida, settlers poached on the land, or tried to; slaves escaped to it; Indians used it as an asylum from their pursuers; Spaniard subjects felt their distant government could not protect them. In all these ways Florida's borders were an irritant that local interests were constantly scratching, calling on the federal government to assert its right of ownership. Late in June 1810, Madison authorized a confidential agent, William Wykoff, to stir up demands within West Florida for America to take possession of the area. "Secretly the administration had authorized an agent to foment revolution in the territory of a friendly nation."[3] This effort seemed to be succeeding on July 27, when a convention of dissident locals in West Florida met at St. John's Plains. But when the forces of this convention stormed Baton Rouge in October and took the Spanish governor captive, they declared West Florida an independent state, willing to negotiate its entry into the American union—the course Texans would follow, later, in their revolt from Mexico.

This was not at all what Madison wanted. His contention was that the area belonged to the United States already; it had been purchased. The transition from Spanish rule to independence would introduce international and congressional obstacles. Since Congress would not be convening until December, and Madison wanted to take over the territory before another nation could intervene, or before land speculators could rush in to get grants from the "independent" power, he issued a proclamation on October 27, sending troops to occupy West Florida as an American possession (P 2.595).[4] It would later be said that he had no constitutional right to do this without congressional authorization (or at all); but that objection could not be immediately lodged, since he kept the proclamation secret in Washington, while sending messengers off to proclaim it in Florida. Madison was trying to create a fait accompli. He would reveal what he had done only in his annual address to Congress, on December 5 (P 3.50).

So much for West Florida. As for East Florida, Madison sent a secret message to Congress on January 3, 1811, asking for authority to seize it should occasion arise. After being given that secret mission, and one hundred thousand dollars to accomplish it, Madison set about creating the occasion for exercising this secret authority. He sent two agents, George Mathews and John McKee, to do for the East what Wykoff had done for the West—foment the conditions for a takeover. They established a base on Amelia Island for carrying this out; but when they could not deliver East Florida, the president refused to recognize them as his agents.[5] West Florida was now partly occupied but without a settled authority, and East Florida still dangled just beyond Madison's reach. Monroe, who had signed the document disowning Mathews and McKee, would finally get East Florida, but only after he had become president.

6

Foreign Affairs: Suckered Twice (1809–1810)

It seemed for a time that Madison would be blessed, early in his first term, with the kind of fortunate break that Jefferson enjoyed with the Louisiana Purchase. Shortly after his inauguration in March 1809, the British representative in Washington, David Erskine, reported that his government was ready to lift the Orders in Council that denied America neutral trading rights with other countries and their colonies. On April 19, the president used an authority given him by Congress to lift the nonintercourse act with whichever country, England or France, first removed its own trade barriers against the United States. Though the proclamation was not to take effect until June 10 (to allow time for promulgating its new trade terms over the ocean and back), six hundred ships left American shores during that interval, confident of free entry by June.

Even Madison's Federalist enemies, along with dissidents in his own party, now vied with each other to praise him. The wisdom of the embargo was retrospectively vindicated. England had been forced to truckle and Madison rubbed in his victory, telling Erskine that the captain of the British ship that had fired with insufficient warning on the USS *Chesapeake* should be handled "with what is due from His Britannic Majesty to his own honor" (R 42)—a suggestion that the king had been dishonorable to that point. The remark caused bitter indignation in England. Jefferson, too, was not magnanimous in victory. He wrote from Monticello:

The British ministry has been driven from its Algerine [pirati-
cal] system, not by any remaining morality in the people, but
by their unsteadiness under severe trial. But whencesoever it
comes, I rejoice in it as the triumph of our forbearing and yet
persevering system. It will lighten your anxieties, take from
cabal its most fertile ground of war, will give us peace during
your time. (P 1.139)

He then warned Madison about any follow-up treaty with the
British: "They never made an equal commercial treaty with any
nation, and we have no right to expect to be the first" (P 1.139).

While the nation was rejoicing at this vindication of neutral trading rights, Madison, following Jefferson's example, left Washington
for a summer break at his own plantation. While he was there, news
began to trickle in from British newspapers that England was *not*
lifting its Orders in Council. Erskine had exceeded his instructions,
omitting three conditions for England's repeal of the Orders,
including a continued right of the British to intercept and board
American ships. Erskine was instantly recalled in disgrace, and it
was announced that Francis James Jackson, a man notorious for
war crimes, was being sent to replace him. The national euphoria
over the end of conflict with England gave way to anger, disbelief,
a desire to punish England, and a sense that Madison had been
gulled.

How had the misunderstanding arisen? As Rutland puts it,
"Madison heard what he wanted to hear" (R 39–40). Not for the
last time, Madison leaped at what he thought *should* be true before
he could verify that it was true. He had predicted all along that
England could not stand up to commercial pressure from America.
Canning's instructions to Erskine tried to excuse British intercep-
tion of American ships bound for France by saying that this was
merely executing Americans' own laws, since Congress had forbidden ships to trade with France in response to Napoleon's Berlin
decree against neutrals. Canning's supposed "concession" was a
denial of American sovereignty over its own ships, and Madison had
taken it as a matter for future discussion, not a hard condition for
suspending the Orders in Council. Erskine let the misinterpretation
stand, in his eagerness to strike an agreement.

It was mere wishful thinking for Madison, like Jefferson before him, to think that the British would give up the right to intercept American ships and to press back into service runaway British sailors. The 1806 treaty that James Monroe had negotiated in London was rejected by President Jefferson because it did not require an end to impressments at sea. But Monroe had good reasons for giving up on that condition. The British navy could not survive if it let its seamen escape to American ships, where they were better paid and flogged less often. The Napoleonic struggle had made control of the sea both difficult and necessary for England. Their press gangs at home had already forced British citizens by the thousands into service.

> During this year [1812] Great Britain had at sea, refitting, or repairing, 191 ships-of-the-line, and 245 frigates and ships of 30 guns, she had several hundred smaller ships-of-war, and she had in hand an extensive building program to increase this force still more. There was a man serving in her fighting fleet for every two hundred men and women and children in her population. And yet this enormous force was stretched very thinly, thanks to Bonaparte's policy of building ships all around the coast of Europe, from Venice to Lubeck. . . . The British Navy continued to expand as fast as ships could be built and men found, somehow, to run them. In seven years its force was almost trebled, at a time when it was generally agreed that nothing less than three years' service was sufficient to train a seaman, and at a time when wastage, from disease, from the accidents of the sea, and from battle casualties was very severe; when the mere lapse of time saw the superannuation of seamen who were understandably too old for their profession at forty.[1]

In the search of American ships for British deserters, some ex-seamen who had become American citizens were taken. In fact, Americans with accents reflecting immigration were taken, too. The United States government was naturally angered by this; but it refused to take steps that would have prevented it. American ships could have refused to hire British subjects. The government could

have issued certificates allowing employment only to American seamen. British deserters could have been quarantined in ports. But
American merchants did not want any of these steps taken. They
depended too heavily on British seamen. When Gallatin surveyed
the overseas commercial trade in 1807, he found that roughly
nine thousand British seamen were engaged in it—over a third of
the overseas crews working under the American flag. Excluding
these workers "would materially injure our navigation" (RL 1446).
Madison, as secretary of state, passed on these findings to President
Jefferson, with a covering comment: "I fear that the number of
British seamen may prove to be rather beyond our first estimate"
(RL 1466). Jefferson responded by calling off any efforts to check
the employment of non-Americans: "Mr. Gallatin's estimate of the
number of foreign seamen in our employ renders it prudent I think
to suspend all propositions respecting our non-employment of
them . . . our best course is to let the negotiation take a friendly
nap" (RL 1469–70).

The merchants whose vessels were being stopped preferred that
invasion of their rights to the drying up of their work pool. But so
long as the United States made no concessions on this employment
of deserters, it was idle to suppose that England would give up
seagoing impressments. "No British ministry that gave up the power
of impressment could last a day" (K 424)—yet Madison for years
maintained the naive belief that the English, under pressure, would
rather give up impressment (that is, give up their fleet) than give up
American trade. He thought that the only thing impeding a recognition of this fact in England was a conspiracy of British coffee and
sugar importers with Caribbean interests, which had blocked England from acting to its larger advantage.

So clear was all this to Madison that he had difficulty accepting
that a "mixture of fraud and folly" could have made it go back on its
word, yielding to the stupid policy of the coffee and sugar men
(P 1.309). Displaying again the insensitivity of the slave owner, he
called this English trickery a greater crime against humanity than
the slave trade: "Such an outrage on all decency was never before
heard of even on the shores of Africa" (P 1.309). Still hoping that
there had been some misunderstanding that would be straightened,
he wrote to Gallatin: "I venture to hope that my return will not be

found necessary" (P 1.25). Gallatin labored to make clear to him the urgency of the situation. "You alone can decide," he signaled in late July. Trying to be tactful, he wrote: "Your return here still seems to me necessary. . . . Whilst I thus press you to come, I write contrary to my personal inclination, for I am extremely desirous to see you in Orange [County during the hot season]" (P. 1.313–14). But he pointedly reminded Madison that Gallatin's own family was being kept in Washington by the crisis.

Popular feeling was running high for punishment of England, but Secretary of State Smith was saying that the president had no power to rescind his April 19 proclamation ending nonintercourse—that was done pursuant to a congressional grant of authority, and no power to reimpose nonintercourse was included in the grant. Still, if the proclamation remained in force until Congress convened again in October, England would continue to be favored, with corresponding injustice to France. Besides, what duties should be charged the British ships now arriving under the favorable rates resulting from the April 19 proclamation? And should the infamous British representative Jackson be received with customary honors—or received at all?

On August 4 Madison submitted to the "mortifying necessity" of dashing back to Washington at the peak of summer, a two-day hard journey without his wife, to cope with developments. The first task was to restore nonintercourse without waiting for Congress. This raised a constitutional problem, the executive's power to undo what Congress had done. Madison had been on both sides of this issue in the past. In the first Congress, he had supported the right of the president to dismiss without Senate approval officers who had been confirmed by the Senate. But then, when President Washington issued his Neutrality Proclamation, undoing a treaty confirmed by the Senate, Madison said that he was exceeding his powers. (Washington argued that the French treaty was made with the *Crown* of France by the American government that preceded adoption of the Constitution—and one or both of those governments had gone out of existence.)

In the new circumstances, Madison said that Congress should have given him the power to reimpose nonintercourse—he had asked it to do that at the time (an admission, here, that they had not done it). He not only made a second proclamation undoing the first. He also created an exception to the congressionally mandated nonintercourse law—British goods imported in the interval between the two proclamations would be charged according to the first, even after it had been repealed by the second. Madison's most admiring biographer describes this sequence of constitutional extensions:

> In substance the President based the validity of the first proclamation on the failure of Congress to take notice of its defects, and based the validity of the second on the defects of the first. He then safeguarded American commerce by orders which presumed the continuing partial effectiveness of the first proclamation after it was superseded. In authorizing British ships to dispose of their cargoes contrary to the provisions of a law just declared to be in full force, the President exercised powers analogous to those of the King in Council. The circular to collectors was the precise counterpart, on this point, of the British disavowal order, which gave American ships sailing under the Erskine agreement a similar protection in British ports. (B 5.78)

Madison's own appointee to the Supreme Court, Joseph Story, felt that he had gone beyond his constitutional powers here. Overruling the proclamation's effect in a circuit case, he said: "I take it to be an incontestable principle that the President has no common law prerogative to interdict commercial intercourse with any nation; or to revive any act whose operation had expired."[2] And even Jefferson had misgivings: "I had doubted [wondered] whether Congress must not be called" (P 1.331).

But Madison issued his proclamation and hurried back to Montpelier, though the arrival of the new minister from England, Francis James Jackson, was expected daily and Gallatin had told him, "I think that a delay in opening communications with Mr. Jackson would be unsatisfactory to the nation as well as prejudicial [to the outcome]" (P 1.313). People wanted an explanation for what had happened; and if Jackson could not supply one in quick order, they wanted him ejected. He was notorious for what had come to be recognized as one of the great war atrocities of the eighteenth century—the leveling of the city of Copenhagen by the British fleet's guns while the nation of Denmark was still considering English demands on it. But Madison let him cool his heels while he completed his summer schedule at home. The disadvantage of this delay was that it left Jackson time to exchange views with Robert Smith, Madison's hapless secretary of state. It was a dialogue of the tactless with the clueless, leaving matters so tangled that when Madison returned he had to insist that Jackson submit his communications in writing, to which Madison himself could compose answers over Smith's name. Jackson naturally took this as an insult to him and his government, but it was at least as much Madison's safeguard against his own government (in the person of Smith).

Another problem with letting Jackson shift for himself was that he had time to explore American society, for which he formed a haughty contempt. His wife, an ex-baroness of Prussia, dismissed her surroundings as barbarian. When the Madisons returned to town, Jackson found the president "plain and rather mean[meager]-looking" and his wife "fat and forty but not fair" (K 467). Jackson and Madison each expected an explanation from the other, and got an accusation instead. Madison wanted to know why the British government had gone back on the offer of its authorized representative. Jackson wanted to know why Madison was naive (or devious) enough to take Erskine's improbable proposal at face value. Like most British ministers (except Erskine), Jackson fell in with Federalist opponents of the administration, and expressed too freely his view that Madison had known Erskine was not following instructions. The president informed him that his communications would no longer be received.

With the failure of the great British breakthrough, Madison was back where he began—or, rather, he was worse off than before. The embargo had failed. The nonintercourse provision that followed had not only failed, but was about to expire. What could be substituted for it, if anything? What would Congress let the president try next? Gallatin, without much hope for his own new proposal, had Nathaniel Macon, as chairman of the proper committee, submit a plan to the House of Representatives on December 19, 1809. It would exclude British and French ships, but not British or French goods carried by other vessels. It was an attempt to keep some revenue from duties while maintaining the opposition to violators of our neutrality. The House and Senate took some things from Macon's bill, added some things to it, and then rejected it on March 16, 1810, just after the end of Madison's first year in office. It was time to start all over again.

Macon submitted another bill as chairman, which became known as Macon's Bill Number 2, though he was neither the author nor a supporter of it. This turned the old nonintercourse logic upside down. The former said that trade was banned with the great powers' ships until one or other power recognized America's neutral rights, upon which trade would be resumed with it. Macon Number 2 said that trade would be *resumed* with both until one recognized neutrality, upon which it would be *withdrawn* from the other. This was a weird form of reverse blackmail, saying in effect, "We will be nice to you both until one is nice in return, upon which we will turn nasty toward the other."

Though the bill was called "miserable feeble puff" at the time (K 499), it gave rise to more wishful thinking on Madison's part. His hopes for accord with England had been based on his belief that England could not do without American commerce. His hope for accord with France was that Napoleon wanted America as an ally against England, a role that Madison was willing to play if that could be done without actually going to war with England. His expectations were unrealistic on both grounds—that Napoleon needed our alliance, and that he would purchase it without obliging us to join with him in war. The mere willingness to entertain offers from Napoleon was an affront to the British, who had an ideology resembling America's in the Cold War. England felt that it was defending the free world against the international tyranny of Bonapartism, their equivalent of Bolshevism. Anyone who was not with them in that struggle was against them; and small nations could be pushed around on the way to getting at the real enemy. Madison's mistake was to take each British shove as proving that America was the main enemy, not merely a little obstacle in the way.

Jefferson had rejected England's claim that it was defending international freedom from Bonaparte, since he thought no monarchy could talk of freedom with a straight face. Besides, he still wanted Madison to coax out of Napoleon a permission to take the Floridas—and even Cuba. He wrote the president: "He will consent to our receiving Cuba into our union to prevent our aid to Mexico and the other provinces" (P 1.140). Madison too was always expecting better treatment from Napoleon than he had any right to; and Napoleon, who had for years been dangling the Republicans between glee and disappointment over the Floridas, now gave them another bait that they swallowed with eagerness.

Napoleon responded to Macon Number 2 on August 2, 1810. He promised to repeal his former bans on neutral trade (the Berlin and Milan Decrees) on November 1, so long as America had imposed nonintercourse with England by then. He made this assurance in a letter issued by his foreign secretary, the Duc de Cadore. When this was delivered to our minister in France, John Armstrong, there had been no discussion of what other measures besides the Berlin and Milan decrees might be observed by Napoleon. He had in fact issued the Decree of Rambouillet in March, which absorbed Holland and authorized the confiscation of American and other ships in all the harbors of his empire. He had no intention of reversing this policy. The mention of Berlin and Milan was a ruse to trap America into conflict with England. And it worked. Thanks to the provincialism and naivete that had been relatively harmless in his prior roles, Madison had been suckered again.

> To say that Madison jumped the gun is too mild. The president threw away all caution and issued a proclamation accepting Napoleon's claims at face value. Unless the British made a similar promise to call off the Orders in Council, a clamp-down on American commerce with Britain would begin in February, 1811. (R 64)

By the time Madison discovered that Napoleon was not observing the terms of Macon Number 2, the bill had done its work. A momentum toward war with England had been accelerated, and would become irreversible, even after England (unlike France) *did* meet the terms of Macon Number 2.

7

Maneuvering into War
(1811–1812)

In the spring of 1811, Madison's presidency seemed stalled in the water. The bank had been dissolved. Reports that France was still seizing American ships suggested that resumption of nonintercourse with England was based on wrong assumptions. William Duane, the editor of the Philadelphia *Aurora*, an Irishman who had spent time in English jails, was calling Madison (of all people) "soft" on England, a man under the spell of the "Frenchified Genevan," Gallatin. Jefferson was pleading with Duane not to desert the president (S 61). Robert Smith, Duane's ally in the cabinet, was telling the British minister that Madison had botched relations with England, and "very different would have been the conduct" of government if Smith were in charge (B 5.274). Not only was Smith feuding with Gallatin in the cabinet, but their wives were berating each other from battling salons (B 5.163). On February 9, Nathaniel Macon had written:

It seems to me not very improbable that Mr. Madison's administration may end something like Mr. Adams's. He may endeavor to go on with the government with men in whom he has not perfect confidence, until they break him down, and then, as John [Adams] did, turn them out after he has suffered all that they can do to injure him. (G 429)

OUSTING SMITH

Gallatin had had enough. On March 5, he submitted his resignation to Madison, who asked him to stay on, assuring him that he was going to get rid of Smith. He directed Gallatin to sound out Monroe (who was now the governor of Virginia) about becoming secretary of state (A 254). It is significant that Madison did not ask this of Jefferson, who had been trying to reconcile Madison and Monroe after Monroe's alliance with John Randolph in the election of 1808. But Jefferson still hoped to do business with the Invisibles, and Madison was finally disillusioned with them. When Gallatin had Monroe's assurance, Madison summoned Smith, recited a list of grievances with him, and demanded his resignation. He would let him save face by appointing him minister to Russia. Smith, after pleading his innocence of all charges, sullenly accepted the Russian commission, but he was soon telling friends it was an "insidious offer" meant to remove him from the scene (B 5.288). He signaled his intent to refuse it by failing to attend a White House dinner for the Russian delegation.

Smith's allies assured him that he had information that could bring down Madison. He believed them, and wrote of the president, "His overthrow is my object and most assuredly will I effect it" (B 5.289). He imagined his power over "the enfeebled mind of our panic-stricken President" (B 5.290). His niece rejoiced that "Jemmy will have hard work to keep in the saddle" (B 5.302). When Duane's *Aurora* indicated that Smith was going to expose the evils of the regime, Jefferson wrote Duane to withdraw monetary support he had been raising in Virginia for the *Aurora* (B 5.295). Smith began the composition of a forty-page pamphlet meant to destroy the government of Madison, which was really the government of Gallatin. But when *An Address to the American People* appeared in the summer, it was the president's foes who were embarrassed by it. Smith presented himself as the lone voice of reason in Madison's cabinet, wisely foreseeing all the flaws in the Macon bills and nonintercourse. He quoted against Madison some State Department documents that Madison had written himself for Smith to sign. He dug up old financial charges from Madison's time as secretary of state. One of Madison's most persistent critics, James

Garnett, wrote about Smith's work to John Randolph: "Singular I call it because it is one of the rare instances of a man's giving the finishing stroke to his own character" (B 5.305). Luckily for Madison, Smith proved as incompetent outside the cabinet as he had been inside it.

Monroe, before accepting Madison's offer to become secretary of state, had demanded that he would be a full partner in the administration, not simply a mouthpiece for Madison's views. This could have meant that Monroe would lead Madison back toward friendly relations with England—Monroe had, after all, struck a treaty with England that would have allowed impressment. But Monroe in fact brought a more warlike attitude into the cabinet. Gallatin always opposed war on economic grounds—America could not afford it, and would lose the Republican ethos if it determined to pay for war by any means available. Jefferson's advice to Madison was always that of a "quaker" who thought reason could find a way to threaten war without ever waging it. Monroe, on the other hand, knew war— he was a hero of the Revolution, who had crossed the Delaware with Washington and been badly wounded at the Battle of Trenton. John Trumbull, who depicted Monroe lying injured on the ground in his famous painting, *The Battle of Trenton*, claimed that the bullet that struck him down later raised him to the presidency.[1] Monroe was young enough at Trenton not to be one of the superannuated Revolutionary generals who would make a mess of the early stages of the War of 1812. He could face war with equanimity, and he steadied Madison's growing determination to wage it.

TIPPECANOE

The prospects for war were strengthened by news from the West, of a clash with Indians manufactured by the governor of the Indiana Territory, William Henry Harrison, who was disturbed by the organizing genius of a Shawnee religious leader, the Prophet, and his warrior brother, Tecumseh. Harrison had negotiated eight Indian treaties for Jefferson, and the Shawnee brothers were uniting people to prevent any further bargaining away of their lands. (They were thought to have murdered some chiefs who signed the treaties.) Like most western governors, Harrison had trouble calling up, organizing, and paying the Indiana militia. He wanted regular troops, and Madison's weak secretary of war, William Eustis, gave him some, ordering that they be used only for defensive purposes. But it was easy for Harrison to take any clash with Indians as an attack calling for a "defensive" counteroffensive. That is what he did while Tecumseh was away in the South organizing the Creek tribes. Harrison took the opportunity to march his troops to Prophetstown on the Tippecanoe River. He camped near the town on November 7, 1811, and left his camp without early-morning lookouts, though that is the time when Indians often attacked. They did so in this case, inflicting and taking heavy casualties. The Indians withdrew when they ran out of ammunition, and Harrison marched into Prophetstown, which had been abandoned overnight. The Prophet had escaped.

Harrison, under criticism from his own men, rushed a self-serving announcement of victory to Washington, and Madison reported it as such on December 18, saying it had brought peace to the frontier (P 4.74). Actually, it brought greater worries—the Prophet and Tecumseh were still active—and more demand for troops from other uneasy governors. When reports began to reach Washington contradicting Harrison's account, Secretary Eustis told Madison it would be bad for military morale to investigate them—though Madison showed his distrust of Harrison in later dealings with him. The legend of Tippecanoe lived on unchallenged, and became a basis for Harrison's successful presidential campaign in 1840.

BACKSTAGE WAR-MAKING

On November 5, shortly before news of Tippecanoe reached Washington, Madison sent to Congress the message he and Monroe had conceived at Montpelier, one that Gallatin tried to soften. It said that British actions "have the character as well as the effect of war" and, in conveying "my deep sense of the crisis in which you are assembled," expressed confidence that "Congress will feel the duty of putting the United States into an armor and attitude demanded by the crisis and corresponding with the national spirit and expectations" (P 4.3). As a follow-up he had the secretary of war ask that ten thousand regular troops be raised. It has often been thought that Madison had war thrust upon him by a Congress controlled by "war hawks" from the West. But Congress was hesitant and doubtful, unwilling to vote for the taxes that would make war preparation a reality. It made some war moves that were actually meant to evade the issue.

The best example of this is its response to Eustis's call for ten thousand regular troops. Senator Giles, who was trying to sabotage Madison and promote DeWitt Clinton for the 1812 election, called that number inadequate, and moved on December 9 to raise twenty-five thousand men. Giles was pushing Madison into a trap, since Republican ideology called for the militia and volunteers to carry the first wave of fighting. Draining volunteers into a standing army was a way to alienate Madison from his base of Republican support, as well as to put an economic squeeze on the administration. The House passed Giles's bill on December 9, 1811, the Senate passed it on January 6, 1812, and the president had to sign it into law on January 7, even though he saw what was being done to him: "With a view to enable the Executive to step at once into Canada, they have provided, after two months' delay, for a regular force requiring 12 [months] to raise it, and after 3 months for a volunteer force on terms not likely to raise it at all for that object" (P 4.168). In response to this complaint, Jefferson, who had criticized Washington for increasing executive powers, regretted legislative meddling with the executive:

> I have much doubted whether, in case of a war, Congress would find it practicable to do their part of the business. That a body containing 100 lawyers in it should direct the measures of a war is, I fear, impossible; and that thus that member of our Constitution which is its bulwark will prove to be an impracticable one from its *cacoethes loquendi* [rabid talking tendency]. It may be doubted how far it has the power, but I am sure it has not the resolution, to reduce the right of talking to practicable limits. (P 4.195)

Some have thought that Madison shilly-shallied his way into war, dragged by others, stalled by doubts. Rutland claims he was little more than a leaf riding the surface of a torrent.

Madison's ignorance of military strategy, his total dependence on generals who had not heard a shot fired in anger for over a generation, and his willingness to go along with public opinion rather than to shape it all suggest that Madison had no firm policy that made war inevitable. Instead, Madison fell into a trap shaped by British inflexibility, pressures from public opinion, and his own gullibility. (R 110)

But Madison created some of the pressures that worked on the public and himself. His readiness, for instance, to seize on the unconfirmed evidence of French cooperation came from his determination to have a showdown with England, to work out his commercial strategy to its logical conclusion.

At times he gave others an impression of indecision, for constitutional and practical reasons. The *constitutional* doubts came from the fact that this would be the first war undertaken after the ratification of the Constitution. The Constitution gives to Congress alone the power of declaring war. There is no specific mention of a presidential role at this stage. The president's power is to conduct the war once it has been declared. Should the president just wait for congressional action, or should he try to guide it? Madison, when trying to limit Washington's ability to use the navy, had written in 1795: "The separation of the power of declaring war from that of conducting it is wisely contrived to exclude the danger of its being declared for the sake of its being conducted" (15.521). The *practical* problem was that Congress might resent intrusion into its prerogative. Madison, largely through Monroe, coordinated ways to choreograph congressional developments. Henry Clay thought he could not guarantee congressional action unless there were some initiative from the executive. But Monroe asked Clay to sound out possible responses to different kinds of pressure (S 96). They were engaged in an elaborate Alphonse-Gaston routine—"*You* first." "No, *you*."

In fact, the maneuvering toward war gave Madison an opportunity to use his old collaborative methods, working with a more public partner. Here his partner was Monroe—and, at one remove, Henry Clay, who was working Congress up to a declaration of war. A good example of Madison's indirect approach was the way he timed the release of dispatches from England, selected for their intransigence, to create indignation in Congress. An even more spectacular, even melodramatic, example was his use of the so-called John Henry letters. In January, just as Congress was authorizing the levy of twenty-five thousand men, an imposter calling himself the Count Edward de Crillon came to Washington and dined frequently at the White House, which was cultivating French connections at this point. "Crillon" told the French minister in Washington, Louis Serurier, that he had some letters of an English spy for sale, letters that might be useful to Madison, since they demonstrated British perfidy in Canada. The spy was named John Henry, and he had been hired by the governor of Canada to explore the possibility of luring New England states back into the empire. Serurier showed samples of the letters to Monroe, who saw their propaganda potential. With Madison's approval, he withdrew fifty thousand dollars from the State Department's discretionary fund to buy them. Then he and the president looked for an opportune time to drop this bombshell on Congress—they did it on March 9, 1812.

In the broad light of congressional skepticism, the letters turned out to be "a dud" (R 90), full of vague allegations easily gleaned from New England newspapers. John Henry was a real Canadian spy for Canada's governor, but what he had turned up was not deemed worth the price he wanted from the Canadians, so he went to England, hoping to sell his goods there. Not having met a buyer, he set sail for America, looking for some more naive customer. On the boat, he met the man posing as Crillon, Paul-Emile Soubiron (P 4.117), who boasted that he could gain access to the highest level of potential purchasers. After getting a letter to introduce "Crillon" from the Republican governor of Massachusetts, Elbridge Gerry (P 4.116), Soubiron became a hit in Washington society, sold the letters, split the money with John Henry, and fled the country. Congress expressed indignation at the amount paid for the worthless letters. "The fifty thousand dollars, which was ultimately wasted, would have paid for a fully fitted frigate for the United States Navy" (R 90). But the letters had at least briefly served Madison's purpose of working up anger against the British rulers of Canada. The episode shows to what extent Madison was working secretly not only with Monroe or the shady count, but with the French minister Serurier, to bring on a war.

Another means Madison used to ratchet up the war spirit was a new embargo, planned by Madison, Monroe, and Clay, and presented to Congress on March 11. The first embargo had been, in Jefferson's mind, a way of preventing war. The new one was, in Madison's mind, a way of preparing for war. Senator Leib of Pennsylvania understood this, but he proposed a longer embargo (ninety days), hoping to stave off the beginning of war long enough for DeWitt Clinton to be elected. Besides building a sense of crisis, the embargo provided a test run for the votes on going to war. In fact, the votes for the embargo were very close to those that were later cast for the war; but some of the earlier votes for the embargo were anti-war votes, meant merely to temporize. The March vote for embargo showed the managers of the war effort what work they had to do before they could risk the June vote for war.

That such background maneuverings were necessary to heat Congress toward a declaration of war became clear when Madison finally asked for that declaration, on June 1 (just before everyone's summer departure from the fetid city). Though the House, under Clay's leadership, quickly passed the declaration (seventy-eight to forty-five), it was a close-run matter in the Senate, which took two weeks of secret session to pass the measure by a vote of eighteen to thirteen. The vote in both houses was purely partisan, no Federalist voting for the war, several Clintonian Republicans voting against it. Madison gave five reasons for going to war with England: 1) impressment, 2) blockades preventing safe departure from the American coast, 3) blockades preventing safe arrival at other shores, 4) confiscation of neutral trade at sea, and 5) the incitement of Indian hostility in the Northwest. The four maritime violations were not new, and were overlapping as he listed them. The Indian hostility was caused more from American expansion than British instigation (the Indians fled to the British from campaigns like that at Tippecanoe), but this grievance had to be listed, in order to bring Henry Clay's western constituents into the effort. Madison, far from being pushed into war by a bellicose Congress, had to drag his own hesitant party into it, past the determined obstruction of the Federalists. What had made Madison, the former pacifist, become a "warhawk"? One thing—Canada.

8

To Conquer Canada
(1812)

Why did America go to war? And why with England rather than with France? French seizures of American shipping were not as common as English harassment, but they were, in principle, the same violations of sovereignty. But Americans had never been the subjects of France. There was special humiliation in any submission exacted by a former master. The new war promised to conclude the unfinished business of the Revolution. Impressment, exclusion from markets, smugglers' ties with Canada, Indian ties with British agents in the West—all these made some chafe as if they were still under the thumb of King George. But none of this would have justified the war unless an easy target seemed to offer itself. England's military force was deeply engaged in the war with Napoleon, which left its western remnant of empire exposed. Canada, it was thought, could be seized before England had the time or spare men and ships to rush aid to it. Once taken, it could be used as a bargaining chip for settling all American grievances, to be restored under terms if at all.

The Canadian delusion was widespread. Jefferson said, "The acquisition of Canada this year [1812] will be a mere matter of marching" (R 110). John Randolph complained of the war debates in Congress: "Ever since the report of the Committee on Foreign Relations came into the House, we have heard but one word—like the whippoorwill, but one monotonous tone—Canada, Canada, Canada" (A 395). Jefferson thought a quick flow of southern militiamen could start the war in the summer—"all declare a preference of a march to Canada"—and they could be spelled in the winter by northerners "acclimated by birth or residence" to the rest of the march that would make Canada ours (P 4.520). Anyone foolish enough to resent this way of stopping the British-inspired "Indian barbarities" could easily be shut up: "A barrel of tar to each state south of the Potomac will keep all in order" (P 4.519). This echoed the glee with which the young Madison imagined opponents of the Revolution being tarred and feathered into submission.

This war euphoria paired a vast overestimation of American military ability with a vast underestimation of Canada's. It was thought that Canada was poorly garrisoned by England and loosely attached to it. Lower Canada contained many French inhabitants, who were presumed to have shaky loyalties if any toward the empire. In December 1811, while the debate over troop levels was crawling through Congress, Secretary of War Eustis sent a secret agent, Benjamin Stickley, to scout the defenses of Canada. In a sketchy memorandum of thirty pages, submitted in February, he confirmed the dreams of easy victory (S 228–29). Quebec, the Canadian capital, was well fortified but thinly manned; Montreal was well manned but thinly fortified. Stickney, the son-in-law of Madison's friend John Stark, was influenced by Republican ideology, which held that standing armies were filled with hired and perfunctory fighters, "much debilitated by intemperance." This encouraged some men's hopes that money for regular troops did not have to be raised, since a great part of the fighting would be done by American yeomen, the militiamen and volunteers. Another result of this optimism about a quick victory in Canada was a vindication of Republican ideology on the subject of navies:

> Congressional niggardliness toward a naval buildup may have been due to Republican lawmakers' delusions. Most of them had a bad case of Canada on the brain, and soldiers, not sailors, would be the conquerors of the British province. From Henry Clay down to the lowliest congressman, the Republicans had convinced themselves that money spent on a navy

was wasted, given that a Canadian invasion would be little more than a few border skirmishes followed by an unconditional surrender. So much for conventional Washington wisdom on the eve of the battle. (R 89)

J. C. A. Stagg has shown how important Canada was in Madison's own war thinking (S 3–47). All through the 1790s, Madison had downplayed the commercial importance of Canada. To advance and defend his plan for the embargo, he had to say that the bulk of England's trade from North America could come only from the United States. Canada's exports were insufficient to make up for an American embargo. When the embargo was canceled, however, Madison performed one of those drastic reversals that mark his career. All of a sudden, Canada became vital to British survival. The United States could now subdue England by taking over Canada and denying *its* products to the empire. This switch was partly based on some real changes in the world situation. Napoleon had cut off much of England's supplies from Europe, so it did depend more on Canada for certain goods, especially for the vast amounts of timber the British fleet required. Madison could not know—though he might have allowed for the possibility—that this situation would be rapidly altered, as it was in 1812, right after Madison went to war, when Napoleon met repulse in both Russia and Spain, and England's old markets were opening up to them again.

But ideology had more to do with Madison's analysis than did the course of events. He found in the new assessment of Canada a way to maintain his idée fixe of three decades, that England could be tamed by commercial pressure. Now the pressure would come after a conquest of Canada—but that initial easy victory would actually *prevent* full-scale war. Britain, feeling helpless without Canadian timber, would finally grant America its rights as a neutral nation. He had changed his estimate of Canada to avoid changing his basic concept. As Stagg puts it, "Madison's decision to wage war for Canada was not basically inconsistent with the diplomacy of peaceful commercial restriction he had advocated prior to 1812" (S 6–7).

The initial war aim, therefore, was to conquer Canada in 1812, before England could reinforce its troops or deploy the fleet to assist them. That schedule had two even closer deadlines built into it—enough progress should have been made by November to assure Madison's re-election, and enough of Canada should be in American hands by December to allow setting up defensible winter quarters there. At a minimum, Montreal should be taken, so the winter pause could be devoted to assembling resources for taking Quebec. As it turned out, no part of Canada was taken in 1812. Rather, Canada conquered the Michigan Territory. The United States had rushed into a war without military staff organization, supply depots, or a credit system worked out for dealing with military contractors. William Eustis, the secretary of war, spent much of his time looking at catalogues for supplying shoes and uniforms. The three generals to whom the invasion was entrusted were not in contact with each other, either directly or through Eustis. Militia and regular troops undercut each other. Mutinies were a constant threat.

DEFEAT IN THE WEST

The logic of the war should have pushed every American effort eastward up the Saint Lawrence River, or north by way of Lake Champlain, toward Montreal—there was even talk of conquering the British naval base at Halifax. But the western sector could not simply be turned over to British and Indian forces. Troops had to be dispatched to the exposed outpost of Detroit, which faced a Canadian fort just across the Detroit River. This meant that the western and eastern armies of the United States were separated by the whole length of Lake Erie and Lake Ontario, bodies of water patrolled by British ships. Communication between the separated American forces was by way of hundreds of miles of difficult land travel. Yet Eustis conceived America's western and eastern armies as mounting a coordinated pincer action, forcing Canada to distribute its thin resources, making it more vulnerable at both ends of the lakes. The Canadians, however, were defending what military theorist Jomini called interior lines, the lakes giving them a mobility denied to the Americans, who were scattered in a great loop around the land routes from the Ohio Territory to Maine. The western army could not even keep a supply line open to its southern recruiting areas of Ohio and Indiana, since marauding Indians cut them off. The forces in the East, meanwhile, could not agree on their own mustering points. It is hard to see how the war could have begun with worse prospects.

William Hull was given the military command in Detroit. He had served throughout the Revolution, reaching the rank of lieutenant colonel in the Massachusetts line. Retired to the practice of law, he was a major general of the Massachusetts militia when Jefferson, in 1805, made him the governor of Michigan Territory. In April 1812, he went to Washington to confer on the defense of his territory in case of war. Madison offered him a commission as brigadier general in the regular army, with two thousand troops for the defense of Detroit. He turned down the offer, saying the force would be insufficient if war came. Madison then offered the same commission to Jacob Kingsbury, who also refused it. Returning to Hull, Madison persuaded him to take the commission; but Hull seems to have thought this was a defense force that would be augmented in case he had to invade Canada.

This was not the first occasion on which the President had used ambiguity as a way of advancing his goals, and he probably hoped that when war was declared Hull would respond to orders to enter Upper Canada. The subsequent problems and ultimate failure of the northwestern campaign, however, all originated in the misunderstandings thus created. (S 193)

Hull was authorized to raise twelve hundred militia troops from Ohio Territory, though he was not empowered to commission their officers in the regular line. He waited with these troops in Cincinnati during the month of May, until regular troops stationed in Indiana Territory could reach him. The joint army then advanced on Detroit by cutting a new road there, which consumed the month of June. Hull, on his arrival at Detroit, was informed of the war's commencement and ordered to attack Fort Malden across the river-border. He did cross the river, to control traffic on it from both sides, but withdrew again before attacking the fort. News reached him on July 29 that the Michigan outpost of Michilimackinac had been captured by Canadian and Indian troops. His new road was also swarming with Indian raiders, denying him logistical support.

In councils of war on what course to take he showed an inability to control the squabbles between militia and regular officers. The militia colonels demanded that their state rank take precedence over lieutenant colonels in the regular army.

Hull, who had suffered a stroke in the preceding year, and who could not even control his horse, seemed cowardly to his officers as he put off the assault on Fort Malden. He sent detachments to reopen the road for reinforcements, but they were beaten back by Tecumseh and his men. The Canadians, who had been shelling Detroit from the opposite shore, now crossed the river and prepared to lay siege on Detroit. Their ultimatum included a threat of Indian massacre, which was clearly preying on Hulls's mind. By this time the Revolutionary veteran had become a blithering idiot:

> Thereafter, possibly under the influence of both alcohol and narcotics, combined with the effects of his earlier stroke, his behavior became increasingly disorganized; his speech became indistinct, he dribbled incessantly, and he took to crouching in the corners of the fort. (S 205)

He surrendered Detroit on August 16, after worrying whether to use a dirty towel or a clean sheet as the white flag. The northwest territory was now exposed to an enemy based on American soil.

In the panic that followed the loss of Michigan, Monroe listened eagerly to suggestions that he rush to the Northwest to lead an army for recapturing Detroit. Jefferson could replace him as secretary of state—an idea Madison rightly rejected (S 209). That would have been like Jefferson's own attempt to call Washington back to Virginia to rescue his foundering governorship. In the darkest hours, Madison never lost his nerve on that scale. But Madison did tell Monroe to go to the Northwest as a volunteer without rank, to take over the regular troops being marshaled under James Winchester: "I see no evil in risking your appointment comparable to that which may be obviated by it. The Western country is all in motion and confusion. It would be grievous if so much laudable ardor and effort should not be properly concentrated and directed."

This plan was aborted by the independent actions of William Henry Harrison, who had already gone outside his Indiana Territory to take command of militiamen from Kentucky and Ohio. He refused to accept a commission in the regular army, since that would have subordinated him to Winchester or to Winchester's replacement, Monroe. He wanted to retain the option of defending the Indiana town of Fort Wayne rather than going to retake Detroit. To protect his independence, he brought along with him six congressmen or ex-congressmen from Kentucky (S 215–16), and commissioned his officers in the militia to command regular troops. Madison had to surrender to the inevitable. Monroe was not sent west, Winchester was ordered to join Harrison's army in a (wholly irregular) subordinate position, and Harrison was asked to retake Detroit in any manner he could devise.

Harrison, while professing that he would end up in Detroit, said he must first protect himself from Indians to his rear by undertaking a sweep of Indian villages. The "hero of Tippecanoe" made himself popular with the frontiersmen who worried more about their longtime Indian foes than about any Canadian campaign. Winter came with no prospect of recapturing Detroit, and a detachment of Winchester's troops was defeated by Indians at the Raisin River. After their surrender, sixty of the Kentucky militiamen were butchered by drunken Indians. Harrison swore to avenge this, but his militiamen's terms of service were up, and he could do nothing but go into winter quarters with his sadly diminished forces.

PARALYSIS IN THE EAST

The raising of the army to drive on Montreal also ran into militia problems. The governors of Massachusetts, Connecticut, and Rhode Island refused to call up their militias for the campaign. Republicans in those states took this as a confirmation of the John Henry letters accusing New England of plotting with the British. Madison decided he could not afford to create an even more fragmented nation by imposing federal law on the governors. He would have to rely on militia from other states. But in New York, the infighting of Republican politicians—they were divided between

Clintonians and anti-Clintonians—led Madison to support a Federalist, Stephen Van Rensselaer, as commander of the militia. Governor Daniel Tompkins reluctantly agreed to this unfortunate decision. Van Rensselaer, making no secret of his disapproval of the war, feared that he was being set up by the Republicans—was being "Hulled" as he put it (accused of cowardice and treason, as Hull was after Detroit's surrender, S 248).

The eastern operations were commanded by Henry Dearborn, who had invaded Canada during the Revolution as part of Benedict Arnold's assault on Quebec. He began mustering troops in Boston, despite the opposition of Massachusetts to the war. He let armies mustering at Buffalo, Albany, and Plattsburgh flounder for lack of leadership, and confused everyone by striking an unauthorized armistice with the governor of Lower Canada on August 8, buying time to assemble his army. The bemused British thought that America was trying to call off the whole war. Madison, as soon as he heard of this, canceled the armistice and told Dearborn to get on with the invasion. The militia troops, disgusted with dithering leaders, began drifting home, claiming it was illegal for them to enter another country.

In New York, Dearborn favored the regular army general from Virginia, Alexander Smyth, over the distrusted militia leader, Van Rensselaer. When Van Rennselaer tried to quiet doubts about his loyalty by leading a brief invasion of the Niagara Peninsula on October 12, parts of his militia refused to go with the invaders, fearing they would be made prisoners in Canada—which is exactly what happened to the advance party that did cross and was left stranded on Queenston Heights, where they had to surrender. Van Rennselaer resigned in disgrace, "Hulled" as he had predicted. Dearborn united Van Rennselaer's New York militia with Smyth's regulars; but after the Virginian insulted the New Yorkers as "an undisciplined rabble," he had to be protected from their wrath by bodyguards. Innkeepers refused to let him stay on their property for fear that his own men would break in to kill him (S 251). "The American army began to disintegrate even as it was still being formed" (S 247).

Dearborn, who had wasted the summer and autumn, decided to cross into Canada on November 19, to set up a winter camp. This would at least let him say that the army was established in Canada by the end of 1812. But his regular troops accidentally fired on the militia during the operation, and the whole body had to retreat in disorder back to American soil, where Dearborn ended the campaign of 1812, the year that was to have witnessed the conquest of Canada.

9

Frigates and a Fresh Start
(1812)

The only bright performance of American fighting men occurred where some least expected it, where British supremacy was universally acknowledged, at sea. The American navy had suffered neglect and insult during Jefferson's eight years as president. The British navy had 191 ships of the line (carrying about sixty to eighty guns). America had none. The British had 245 frigates (about thirty to fifty guns). America had 7, of which only 6 would see action during the war. The disproportion was so ludicrous that the drunken secretary of the navy wondered if there was any point in letting his puny force sail. Yet the first American victories—for a long time the only ones—were at sea. They alone redeemed the war effort during the year 1812, and they helped Madison win reelection in the fall.

The ships and the seamen of the war's early days have kindled a fondness in their celebrants—Henry Adams, Theodore Roosevelt, Alfred Thayer Mahan, C. S. Forester. Partly this comes from the fact that the War of 1812 was the last one fought under sail, before the coming of steam. It climaxed the sea exploits of the Napoleonic era. But the praise, both for the men and for the ships, is well deserved. Americans had a secret asset—the genius of a Quaker naval architect named Joshua Humphreys. They also had crews and captains of great ingenuity and daring.

THE HUMPHREYS FRIGATES

If Jefferson had been able to get his way, America would have possessed no frigates at all in 1812. The great frigates, built by the Federalists during Washington's administration, had been strenuously
opposed by the Republicans in Congress. Gallatin, then a congress-
man from Pennsylvania, tried to prevent their construction. After
they were constructed he tried to prevent their being fitted and
manned (G 169–72). "The founding of the United States Navy was
a political act, even a partisan act, the work of the Federalist Party."[1]
Madison's record on the navy, as on so many things, was inconsistent, his later Republicanism warring with his early Federalism. We
have already seen how, in the Continental Congress, he advocated a
peacetime navy for building national unity: "If a naval armament
was considered as the proper instrument of general government, it
would be both preserved in a respectable state in time of peace, and
it would be an object to man it with citizens taken in due proportion from every state" (3.72). In *The Federalist* Number 41, he
spoke pseudonymously as a New Yorker on the need of that state
for a navy, showing "the palpable necessity of the power to provide
and maintain a navy":

> If we except perhaps Virginia and Maryland, which are pecu-
> liarly vulnerable on their Eastern frontiers, no part of the
> Union ought to feel more anxiety on this subject than New
> York. Her seacoast is extensive. The very important district of
> the state is an island. The state itself is penetrated by a large
> navigable river for more than fifty leagues. The great empo-
> rium of its commerce, the great reservoir of its wealth, lies
> every moment at the mercy of events and may almost be
> regarded as a hostage for ignominious compliances with the
> dictates of a foreign enemy, or even with the rapacious
> demands of pirates and barbarians.

Speaking in his actual state, at the Virginia ratifying convention, he
said that only a navy could protect America's neutral rights if (for
instance) France and England should be at war.

We need not expect, in case of such a war, that we should be
suffered to participate in the profitable emoluments of the
carrying trade unless we were in a respectable situation. . . . I
did not contend that it was necessary for the United States to
establish a navy for that sole purpose, but instanced it as one
reason out of several for rendering ourselves respectable.[2]

In the 1790s, Madison would turn this argument on its head,
using the same evidence to argue *against* possessing a navy. By that
time he had joined Republican opposition to a navy for fighting
Algerine pirates. Precisely *because* (in his conspiratorial view) the
English were stirring up the pirates to take American commercial
ships (M 15.514), it would be fatal to send warships to the
Mediterranean—"sending ships of force among the armed powers
would entangle us in the war if anything would do it" (15.263).

If there were any disposition in Great Britain to be irritated
into a war with us, or to seek an occasion for it, those who, on
other questions, had taken that ground of argument ought to
be particularly aware of danger from the collision of naval
armaments within the sphere of British jealousy. (15.531)

The idea of fighting in Tripoli seemed to him quixotic: "The frigates
at so great a distance, on a turbulent sea, would be exposed to dan-
gers, as well as attended with expenses, not to be calculated"
(15.530).

Was Madison content, then, to let British insults go unrequited?
No, of course not. By this time (1795) Madison had invented his
real weapon, commercial blackmail. If Britain does not control the
pirates, America will simply stop selling that nation the goods it
needs. He argued

that Great Britain was more vulnerable in her commerce than
in her fleets and armies; that she valued our necessaries for her
markets, and our markets for her superfluities, more than she
feared our frigates or our militia; and that she would, conse-
quently, be more ready to make proper concessions under the
influence of the former than of the latter motive. (15.519)

While the Federalists were calling for six frigates, Madison tried to limit them to two or three.[3] When Congress authorized all six, he argued that the president had no constitutional right to use the ships for any purpose other than protection from piracy: "The sole and avowed object of the naval armament was the protection of our trade against the Algerines. To that object the force is appropriated by the law itself. The President can apply it to no other" (15.532).

When Jefferson was elected president, he tried to put the obnoxious frigates in drydock; but by then their use in the Mediterranean had become effective and popular. He sent four of the six to besiege Tripoli, where they exacted from the Pasha the Treaty of 1805. But meanwhile Jefferson was installing a program meant to retire the frigates from service. Gallatin, as secretary of the Treasury, was now in a position to undo a navy whose existence he had opposed in the first place. All that was needed, in Republican policy, were a few ships for coastal defense. Any farther naval reach should be precluded. Jefferson had his own dreams of empire, but they were not to include a seagoing navy. He hoped to add Cuba to his "empire of liberty," but that would not break his rule: "Cuba can be defended by us without a navy, and this develops the principle which ought to limit our views. Nothing should ever be accepted which would require a navy to defend it" (P 1.140). Cuba could be defended, like the mainland's coast, by gunboats.

Gunboats were to Jefferson what commercial pressure was to Madison—a magic solution. The boats were clever shortcuts, like Jefferson's labor-saving inventions at Monticello (which cost more labor than they saved in constant repair). The gunboat was nothing but a floating platform mounted with one gun at the bow. It thus offered a slim profile as a target, and a row of gunboats could be drawn across a harbor like a movable artillery battery. They were not seaworthy, so they could only be used in defense, not offense. They were only to be brought into position when a harbor was under attack, so they could be stored most of the time, with no expense of maintaining a crew or a complement of gunners.

The attraction of this for Gallatin was that gunboats were, comparatively, cheap. But Jefferson was so enthusiastic about the project that he wanted two hundred of them. Trying to cut that number to seventy-three, Gallatin wrote: "Of all the species of force which

war may require—armies, ships of war, fortifications, and gunboats—there is none which can be obtained in a shorter notice than
gunboats, and none therefore it is less necessary to provide beforehand" (G 352). But Jefferson demanded the full two hundred:
"When he fairly mounted a hobby-horse, he rode it over all opposition, and of all hobby-horses gunboats happened at this time to be
his favorite" (G 353).

The gunboats proved to be ineffective, expensive, and an obstacle
to building and manning real ships. Gallatin had opposed a large
fleet of them since "they will inevitably decay in a given number of
years, and will be a perpetual bill of costs for repairs and mainte-
nance" (G 353). He was understating the problem. Left alone, they
rotted in a year. Real seamen did not want to serve on them—they
did not even give steady employment, much less the chance for
prize money that seagoing ships promised. They were unstable in
turbulent water—the guns had to be dismounted and put low in
the hold or they would capsize. It proved easy to sink or seize them.
In the War of 1812, frigates and sloops and privateer ships all performed gloriously. Gunboats were useless, and the secretary of war
would order them destroyed.

George Washington's original six frigates were James Madison's
best war weapon in the year 1812—USS *Chesapeake, Congress,
Constellation, Constitution, President,* and *United States.* They had
all seen service in the Tripolitan wars or in the Quasi-War, where
they won the surprised admiration of established navies. The
frigates were technological marvels, the most advanced fighting
ships of their time. They had been created by Joshua Humphreys,
who overcame his Quaker reservations about war to perform the
patriotic act of giving the nation this resource. (When other countries tried to secure his services, he turned them down.) Since
Republican opposition to the navy had ruled out building any ships
of the line—the juggernauts of the day, meant (as their name indicated) to fight in line of battle, with massive firepower—Humphreys
came up with the concept of a superfrigate, one that met the congressional requirement of the ship's class, but which nonetheless
carried more men (up to 450), more guns (up to fifty-four), more
armor in the hulls, and more sail than ordinary frigates. The extra

number of men was important, for boarding enemy ships during combat and for manning prize vessels after their capture.

Despite these additions to their weaponry, the Humphreys ships were faster and more maneuverable than other frigates. Their guns were ingeniously disposed, mounted on one deck, not two. They were fast enough to cut ships out of British convoys, fight them down, and slip away. C. S. Forester claims that Humphreys "instilled a living force into his fighting machines."[4] To create a *national* pride in them, to spread employment, to speed their completion, they had been built simultaneously in different port cities after Congress authorized their construction in 1794. Humphreys himself built the *United States* in Philadelphia, and other naval architects worked to his designs in Portsmouth, Boston, New York, Baltimore, and Norfolk. Of the Humphreys frigates only one saw no service in the War of 1812. The *Constellation* was undergoing repairs in Norfolk when the war began, and by the time it became seaworthy, the British fleet had sealed up Chesapeake Bay, leaving the ship no path out to the sea. This was an important loss, since the ship had won two famous victories against French vessels in the Quasi-War.

USS PRESIDENT

The difference between the land and sea forces in this war can be seen from the fact that the leading generals, at the outset, were near or over sixty years old, while ship captains were under forty. Sea command demands constant and immediate control, unlike land war, where the general can be at some distance from the frontline fighting. The generals in 1812 found excuses for not fighting, while the ships ran ahead of orders into the fight. Two Humphreys frigates—*President* (captain John Rodgers) and *United States* (captain Stephen Decatur)—were in New York when war was declared on June 18. As soon as news of the declaration reached the city, they cleared harbor (June 24), along with smaller ships brought with them to scout for prey. By doing this they eluded British ships being sent to seal up the New York harbor. John Rodgers, the commodore of this squadron, had been a captain since the age of twenty-eight, when he ran a prize ship home after its defeat by the *Constellation* in the Quasi-War. Even before the War of 1812 began, he had commanded *President* when it attacked the British sloop *Little Belt*, mistaking it near nightfall for the marauding frigate *Belvidera*.

Out now with his squadron in the first days of the declared war, he spotted the real *Belvidera* and badly crippled it; but a gun exploded under the deck Rodgers was standing on, breaking his leg, and the *Belvidera* escaped. This turned out to be a fortunate accident, since the *Belvidera* limped into Halifax, where Vice Admiral Henry Sawyer commanded all the British ships in American waters. He had planned to disperse his frigates along the American coast, to block access to its ports; but news that Rodgers was at sea with a squadron made Sawyer unwilling to spread his forces so thin. But for that, there would have been a British detail waiting to intercept the *Constitution* when it arrived in Boston harbor after an exhausting escape on July 26, or when it sailed out again with new supplies on August 2.

Rodgers searched in vain for a British convoy to attack, and put in at Boston after ten weeks at sea without taking a major prize. But Forester argues that this was a tremendously important cruise:

> Rodgers knew that during these last few weeks, with the imminent approach of war, American merchant vessels had begun to swarm home, and part of his manifold duty was to ensure their safe entry into American harbors, and he had to do this in the face of a manifestly superior force. His disappearance out to sea with his united squadron was the most effective way of ensuring this. No single British cruiser would gladly remain at a focal point off the American coast when the captain was aware that at any moment Rogers's topsails might appear over the seaward horizon, cutting him off from escape; no British admiral would gladly have his cruisers dispersed in situations inviting their destruction in detail. With Rodgers's departure known, there would be urgent British orders for concentration. The net cast to entrap American shipping would be entirely altered in character; the individual strands would have to be made stronger, at the cost of making the holes infinitely larger—so large that in the event the homeward bound shipping made its escape with remarkably

small loses. Rodgers's bold decision to take his squadron far out to sea had a profound effect on the rest of the war.[5]

USS CONSTITUTION

When Rodgers arrived at Boston harbor on August 31, it was to a city glowing with pride in the exploits of the *Constitution*. That ship had put to sea from Annapolis on July 5. With winds of any energy, a Humphreys frigate could speed away from any ship of its class. But there was little or no wind on July 17, when a large British squadron of three frigates and a ship of the line appeared in the late afternoon and took up the pursuit of the *Constitution*. Captain Isaac Hull (nephew of the William Hull about to be disgraced at Detroit) tried to sail away during the night, but found the ships closer to him at sunrise. With no wind power, he sent out boats to haul his ship with their oars. The British did the same, but they had an advantage. They signaled for boats from their slower frigates, to supply their lead frigate with a dozen teams of rowers. Then Hull sent boats to row swiftly ahead for half a mile, where they could plant a kedge anchor. As winches on the *Constitution* drew the ship to that anchor, other boats were moving ahead to plant their kedges in sequence. The British followed suit. For two days and two nights this laborious chase ground on, suspended only when a slight wind came up, at which point Hull would hoist buckets of water to the yardarms for wetting the sails, making them more sensitive to any breeze.

Then came the lightest of breezes, and Hull set all sail. The most careful organization and good seamanship were required to get in the boats while the ship was under way; with the enemy only half a mile out of range, an accident could be fatal, especially as a pursuer could well, if an opportunity presented itself, leave a boat behind him to be picked up by a following friendly ship. . . . Then the breeze died away to nothing, the ships all lying motionless on a glass sea in the growing heat of the July sun. Out went the boats again, and the dreadful toil at the oars recommenced.[6]

Hull had to time the relays of men on duty to keep up this grueling marathon for over fifty hours. He also had to decide when it was absolutely necessary to pump out the drinking water—ten tons of it—to lighten the ship. After that, there would be no wetting the sails. A merciful final storm arose and swept him into Boston harbor, where this exploit became an instant legend for giddy celebration.

This was one of the many paradoxes of the navy's status. It remained the darling of the Federalists, even though they were opposed to this war. One reason Jefferson disliked the navy was that it came from the mercantile classes of the North, from men who had made and sailed the whalers and smuggling ships— rootless improvisers totally unlike the sturdy yeomen of the soil that Jefferson idealized. Theodore Roosevelt had an opposite ideal, glorying in the fact that American seamanship was born of the entrepreneurial spirit:

> Wherever an American seaman went, he not only had to con-
> tend with all the legitimate perils of the sea, but he had also
> to regard almost every stranger as a foe. Whether this foe
> called himself pirate or privateer mattered but little. French,
> Spaniards, Algerines, Malays, from all alike our commerce
> suffered, and against all our merchants were forced to defend
> themselves. The effect of such a state of things, which made
> commerce so remunerative that the bolder spirit could hardly
> keep out of it, and so hazardous that only the most skillful
> and daring could succeed in it, was to raise up as fine a set of
> seamen as ever manned a navy. . . . There could not have
> been better material for a fighting crew than cool, gritty
> American Jack.[7]

The American fleet, small as it was, needed no press gang to fill its crews. There was not a split between regulars and volunteers aboard it, as in the land armies. The officers were not appointed because of service decades ago in the Revolution. They were under forty, not over sixty. They were reassessed after each cruise, the successful ones going out again on different ships while the one they brought back was being cleared of barnacles, refitted, and restocked. Soon such men on such ships had more to boast of than an epic escape.

Isaac Hull loved the *Constitution*, which he had served on as a lieutenant during the Quasi-War. It had not been at sea long, its hull was not fouled, it needed no repairs, just re-supply. Knowing that if he took it into the navy yard he would be sent to another ship, he stood out in the harbor and had supplies brought to him, so he could take the ship back out without receiving orders to assume a new command. On August 19 he spied the *Guerriere,* a British frigate that had been terrorizing merchant ships. The expert artillery work of the *Constitution* so riddled the *Guerriere* that Hull could not take it into harbor for refitting as an American warship. He had to blow up the hulk. It was in this fight that the tough Humphreys layering of the ship's hull earned the *Constitution* its nickname, "Old Ironsides."

These early victories were followed by others. The American sloop *Wasp* took the British brig *Frolic* on October 17. Decatur's *United States* captured the *Macedonian* on October 25 and brought it into harbor, the only British frigate saved to be converted to American use. On December 13, the *Constitution,* now under the command of William Bainbridge, destroyed the British frigate *Java.* Over and over the British navy was being given a bloody nose. These victories could not shake British domination of the ocean; but they were as disturbing to the British as they were unexpected. "During the six months the war had lasted, the little United States navy captured three British frigates, besides the twenty-gun *Alert* and the eighteen-gun *Frolic;* privateers by scores had ravaged British commerce, while the immense British force on the ocean had succeeded only in capturing the little *Nautilus,* the twelve-gun brig *Vixen,* and the *Wasp*" (A 565).

RE-ELECTION

The disastrous beginning of the war had less effect than might have been expected on Madison's re-election in November, even though Madison told Jefferson it would "bring the popularity of the war, or of the administration, or both, to the *experimentum crucis* [decisive test]" (RL 1705). The *Constitution*'s exploits boosted morale. The West, which had suffered Hull's loss of Detroit, was itching for revenge, which made it support the war more than any other region. Harrison's uniting of volunteers from Kentucky, Ohio, and Indiana to fight the Indians was popular. Harrison kept military operations in his own hands, while getting political support from Henry Clay in Washington. The result of this was an influx of federal funds, reluctantly doled out by Gallatin, to local banks whose credit needed boosting for the supply of troops. This, reported Samuel Huntington from the West, "tended to consolidate the friends of Mr. Madison's measures long after they ceased to have any personal attachment to the man" (S 219).

Madison tried to blunt opposition to the war in New England by choosing as his vice-presidential running mate Elbridge Gerry, to replace George Clinton, who died in April. But Gerry had just been ousted as governor of Massachusetts, despite his redrawing of electoral districts to promote his re-election (a salamander-shaped district led to the term "gerrymander"). Nothing could make New England support the war. Yet the Federalists were so confined to that area that they supported the anti-Madisonian Republican, DeWitt Clinton, rather than putting up their own candidate. Clinton ran a patently dishonest race, opposing the war in the North but calling for better management of it in the Middle States. Despite this fraudulence, he made the race a tight one. Madison eventually won the electoral count 128 to 89; but it took a month of close counting to establish his win in Pennsylvania. If he had lost its twenty-five votes, Clinton would have beat him.

Madison waited until December, when his electoral victory was assured, to do the belated and badly needed re-organizing of his cabinet and military establishment. Jefferson was just voicing what was common knowledge when he told Benjamin Rush that "so wretched a succession of generals" had never been seen (R 122). Henry Clay, who helped Madison bring on the war, did not place the responsibility for failure on the generals, but on their superior, the president: "Nature has cast him in too benevolent a mould. Admirably adapted to the tranquil scenes of peace, blending all the mild and amiable virtues, he is not fit for the rough and rude blasts which the conflicts of nations generate" (R 119). For Madison to make a fresh start on the war, he would have to rid himself of his bumbling war secretaries, beginning with the hapless Paul Hamilton in the Department of the Navy.

Though the sailors were the only fighters who had distinguished themselves, that success had little to do with Hamilton—a point brought forcibly home to Madison in the week leading up to Christmas. At a White House party, Hamilton's son graciously presented Dolley Madison with the flag of the *Macedonian*, captured by Stephen Decatur in the *United States*—a ceremony undercut by the presence of the secretary himself in his usual intoxicated state (R 119–20). Hamilton, too inept to recognize his own ineptness, tried to hang on when Madison asked for his resignation, and the president had to tell him bluntly that Congress would not authorize any of his requests for navy funds if he remained. Madison had waited too long, just as with Robert Smith; and Hamilton, too, used his inside knowledge to accuse the president of betraying him. He was replaced with a friend of Gallatin from Pennsylvania, William Jones—though Jones disappointed Gallatin by trying to increase funds for a navy that the secretary of the Treasury was still opposed to.

Replacing Eustis as secretary of war was a trickier matter. Since Monroe had wanted to take over the military command of the Northwest, finding too little to do as secretary of state when the nation had given up diplomacy for the duration, Madison offered him the post that would put him in charge of all the armies. Monroe was at first disposed to take the job; but his son-in-law and political adviser, George Hay, advised him not to, on the grounds that it would hurt his ultimate plan of becoming president. It was probably impossible to make a success of the War Department. Gallatin had persuaded Congress that it could continue the war only by scaling it back and extending its timetable, offering the unpalatable prospect of a protracted war, bound to grow even more unpopular as it was extended. Jefferson would soon be writing to Monroe from Monticello, "We must prepare for interminable war" (A 1092). Monroe therefore told Madison that he could serve only temporarily while the president searched for a permanent secretary.

This left Madison with few candidates. He was being told that even his preference for Monroe raised complaints about forging a Virginia dynasty; yet he could not balance the cabinet with a Federalist or a New Englander, since they opposed the war. And the pool of Republicans was narrowed by the level of dissidence in his own party. He had to settle for a man he did not trust, and whom Monroe detested, John Armstrong. During the Revolution, Armstrong had been a leader of the incipient rebellion of military officers at Newburgh. The Republicans later accepted a man thus disgraced in the Federalists' eyes, and Jefferson had sent him as minister to France, whence he relayed to Madison the Cadore letter that became the occasion of the present war. Madison regretted trusting Armstrong on that letter's reliability, and feared that Armstrong had been positioning himself to run for president. Unable to find an alternative, however, he offered Armstrong the post. This meant that the feuding of his first cabinet (Gallatin against Smith) would be replicated in his second one (Monroe against Armstrong). Monroe was especially distrustful when Armstrong took his duty to entail service at the front, where military glory might be won. Monroe spied on Armstrong in his absence, opening his official correspondence, a practice that angered Madison when he heard of it—a clerk in the War Department said the president was "more in a passion than I ever saw him at any other period of his life" (S 369). Madison had made a fresh start after his re-election, but it was not an auspicious one.

III.

The Presidency:
Second Term (1813–1817)

10

Peace Overtures and
Professionalism
(1813–1814)

While Madison was trying to reform the war effort, he was also seek-
ing a way out of this ruinously expensive and unsuccessful endeavor.
The British had been astonished that America initiated hostilities,
and thought it might all be a misunderstanding—Madison's declara-
tion of war crossed the ocean one way while cancellation of the
Orders in Council was crossing it the other way. England took
Dearborn's unauthorized armistice in August 1812 as a signal that
America was having second thoughts, and it offered to negotiate.
But when Madison's representative in London said that an end to
impressment had to be added to the rescission of the Orders, Lord
Castlereagh answered that this was unthinkable. Six months later,
however, in the spring of 1813, Madison was ready to soften his
stand. When Tsar Alexander of Russia, anxious to keep his alliance
with England and to resume trade with America, offered to negotiate the conflict, Madison not only accepted the offer but instructed
his peace commissioners to promise, for the first time, that the
United States would give up using British seamen on its ships and
would surrender those who had deserted, without the need for
searches at sea.

Without waiting for assurance that Britain had accepted the
Russian offer, Madison chose three peace commissioners to repre-
sent America in Saint Petersburg—John Quincy Adams (who was
already at the tsar's court as United States minister), Gallatin, and

the Federalist James Bayard. Madison's desire to escape the war he had brought upon himself is indicated by the fact that all three of these men, without actively opposing the war, had been critical of it (S 301). They would try very hard to find a way of calling it off. But two things went wrong with this delegation, one minor and one fatal. The minor one was the refusal of Congress to confirm Gallatin's appointment (which had been made during a congressional recess)— the French-speaking Gallatin was thought to be too favorable to Napoleon. The fatal problem was England's refusal to take any part in the process. It had no reason to negotiate, given its dominant position in the spring of 1813.

1813: MILITARY SETBACKS

America's original war plan was right in its basic assumption, that Canada should be taken rapidly, before the British could use its fleet to bring reinforcements or to deploy itself along the East Coast. In the spring of 1813, that whole assumption was defunct. Most ports except those in New England had now come under a British blockade—the exemption for New England encouraged Federalist merchants to keep up their forbidden trade with the enemy. A fleet in Chesapeake Bay was increasingly bringing the war home to Madison's fellow Virginians. During the summer, Rear Admiral Sir George Cockburn became the British officer most hated in America, for his raids up the rivers feeding into the bay, where he seized supplies and burned villages.

Stephen Decatur's frigate *United States* and his converted prize ship *Macedonian* were sealed up in New York harbor for the rest of the war. The *Constellation* remained blockaded in Norfolk. When Captain James Lawrence rashly took the *Chesapeake* out of Boston harbor, it was captured and taken in triumph to the British station at Halifax. The wounded Lawrence's words, "Don't give up the ship," became a famous slogan, but that was poor compensation for the loss of one of the original Humphreys frigates. The *Constitution* did not make its way out from the blockade until the last weeks of 1814. The *President* and the *Congress* were at sea, but fought no warships. The heady days of bloodying the British navy's nose were over. Sloops and privateers from America played havoc with British commercial vessels, but so far as war vessels were concerned, Britannia ruled the seas. The American navy's next moment of glory would occur on Lake Erie; but that did not come until the autumn of 1813.

War on land offered no consolation for these setbacks. As secretary of war, John Armstrong showed his political approach to the conflict by deciding that some victory, any victory, had to be scored by Dearborn's army before the April elections for congressional and state offices (S 286). This deadline ruled out a major assault on Montreal, the only objective that made strategic sense; so Armstrong turned his eyes toward a more modest target, Kingston, at the east end of Lake Ontario. But Dearborn's timidity made him look even farther west, to the other end of the lake, to the village of York (present Toronto). Dearborn felt that he could sail there, when the ice melted, on ships that Isaac Chauncey had been building through the autumn and winter for use on the lake. Though the ice was slow to melt in 1813, and the victory at York had to be announced in election handbills before it occurred, the village was taken on April 27. As usually happened on battle days, Dearborn was too ill to lead his own troops and the task was given to Colonels Zebulon Pike and Winfield Scott (Pike died in the assault). Small as York was, it held the capitol of Upper Canada. The fact that Dearborn's troops burnt it to the ground supplied a precedent for what would happen the next year in the District of Columbia.

Dearborn's forces, now led by Winfield Scott, next took Fort George, at the northern end of the Niagara peninsula, but failed to pursue the retiring British force. When two generals, John Chandler and Levin Winder, were sent to attack British detachments on the northern shore of the lake, they were separated from their own forces and captured at the Battle of Stony Creek (June 6). The Canadian campaign had fallen apart, and General Dearborn was held in contempt by the men he was supposed to command.

When Congress met in May, Madison in his frustration had recourse to his favorite remedy for what ailed the nation, embargo. He asked for a ban on trade, since New England was brazenly responding to the lack of a blockade, not only sending out its ships to England but selling grain across the Canadian border to enemy troops. The Congress defeated Madison's proposal. It did more. It asked for the record of diplomatic exchanges with France, to see if Madison had known that Napoleon's Cadore letter did not express his real intent. The newspaper of the administration, the *National Intelligencer,* wrote in a huff: "Search annals of the councils of any free people [to find] not a single precedent in which such a freedom bordering upon rudeness had been exhibited to the chief magistrate of a nation" (R 130). The obvious precedent was Madison's own demand that President Washington turn over the record of negotiations for the Jay Treaty. In June, when freshman senator Daniel Webster, a harsh opponent of the war, took the demand for the French records to Madison, the president was in his bed with a raging fever, "his nightcap on his head," too weak to leave Washington for his summer stay at Montpelier. In fact, he was close to death.

Dolley Madison wrote of this June crisis: "It has been three weeks since I have nursed him night and day. Sometimes I despair!" (B 6.188). Madison's appearance during the height of the fever frightened those who saw him. The *Federalist Republican* wrote that they "have left his chamber under a full conviction of the derangement of his mind" (B 6.210). Since Gerry, the vice president, was also chronically ill (he would die before completing his term), Monroe told Jefferson that some were hoping to make William Giles, as president of the Senate, succeed them after their serial deaths (A 662).

Madison recovered enough, by the end of July, to retire to Montpelier, where he received the cheering news of an American victory in the Northwest. It was fought at the west end of Lake Erie, where Oliver Hazard Perry had been constructing a shallow-draft navy all through the summer, using pegs for nails, mounting on the decks any guns he could collect from Pittsburgh. He was aided in this by the master naval architect Noah Brown. Perry brought a higher level of professionalism than had been seen so far in the Canadian campaigns. The son of a sea captain, he had served on his father's frigate during the Quasi-War, and fought under Rodgers at Tripoli. On Lake Erie (September 10, 1813) he took out his nine ships of various size to meet six British ships under the command of Robert Barclay. Perry's command ship, carrying twenty guns, was named the *Lawrence,* since news had recently reached him of the death of his comrade, James Lawrence, in the defeat of the frigate *Chesapeake.*

He had Lawrence's words, "Don't give up the ship," put in white letters on a large blue flag. When the second ship of his flotilla, the *Niagara*, held back from the conflict, Barclay's principal vessels, the *Detroit* and the *Queen Charlotte*, with nineteen and seventeen guns respectively, trained their batteries on the *Lawrence* and battered its hull, cutting the crew down. (These shallow-draft ships had no quarters below where the wounded could escape fire.)

With most of his crew dead or wounded, Perry gathered his blue flag, entered a boat (luckily uninjured in the general ruin), and rowed to the *Niagara*. The British captains thought the engagement over, and were attaching the hulk of the *Lawrence* to be towed when Perry brought the *Niagara* across their bows to deliver a raking fire (the deadliest angle for a barrage). He, along with the smaller ships in his flotilla, won the engagement, and Perry sent a message to the land troops: "We have met the enemy and they are ours." Perry had plunged into battle under one slogan and emerged creating another. With Lake Erie now controlled by Americans, Perry took Harrison's troops across the lake, on October 5, to attack a force of British and Indians at the Thames River, killing (among others) the great Indian leader Tecumseh. The West was now secured. To the south, Andrew Jackson was beginning his campaign against the Creek Indians, who had been stirred up by Tecumseh in the preceding year.

In the East, on the shore of Lake Ontario, the situation was not so promising. With Dearborn disgraced, the secretary of war decided to go north and take personal command of the situation. He brought up from New Orleans his old comrade from the Revolution, James Wilkinson, to be one instrument in this effort, not realizing that Wilkinson was always a tool that turned in the hand of its wielder. The Spanish had learned that after he took their bribes and betrayed them. So had Aaron Burr. Jefferson should have learned it, but refused to. Now it was Armstrong's turn. Wilkinson was asked to coordinate an attack on Montreal with General Wade Hampton; but these two men despised each other, and each shirked his part of the task, blaming the other. When Wilkinson at last entered the St. Lawrence River on November 5, he had a fever and diarrhea, which he treated with large doses of alcohol and laudanum. "Thus drugged and out of his mind and causing much embarrassment to his officers and doctors, who eventually appealed to Armstrong to relieve him of his command, Wilkinson became 'very merry, and sung, and repeated stories'" (S 3435).

At Chrysler's Point, on November 11, twelve hundred of Wilkinson's three thousand men attacked a British force of eight hundred advancing on their rear, and were routed—in what Henry Adams calls the least creditable showing of the war (A 753). Wilkinson sent out a call for Hampton to join him, but Armstrong had already confused things by opening a winter camp, to which Hampton had retired. Wilkinson retreated back across the New York border, where he ordered Hampton arrested, accusing him of drunkenness. The generals had sailed, and marched, and threatened to fight (more each other than the enemy), and had finally done nothing.

The year 1813 ended with a British invasion of New York. In December, the Americans retired from Fort George to American territory, burning two Canadian towns (Newark and Queenston) in their passage. By way of reprisal, the British attacked Fort Niagara on American soil, killing sixty-seven, most of them bayoneted. Indian raiders were sent across the border. British troops, with their Indian allies, attacked and burned Black Rock and Buffalo on December 29. There was terror throughout all of upper New York as the new year began. Madison would soon be asked to allow the recruitment of Indians to fight on the American side, but he was not panicked into reciprocating atrocities.

1814: NEW ENGLAND RESISTS

At the end 1813, Madison, like an addict, returned to his favorite drug. He called for another embargo, the third he had proposed in the last two years. This time Congress gave him what he wanted, and the New England states interpreted this as a declaration of war on them. When the Massachusetts legislature (the General Court) convened in January, Governor Caleb Strong addressed it, saying that the guilt for all the suffering of war "is chargeable upon that government which unreasonably begins the conflict." The Massachusetts Senate responded that it could "give no encouragement to a war of such a character." Its House of Representatives said that unless Madison showed a true willingness to make peace, it could not offer any support for his war (A 907–8). Forty Massachusetts town meetings sent petitions to the General Court, demanding that it "put an end to this hopeless war" (Amherst) or promising that "we profess ourselves ready to resist unto blood" (Newbury). The General Court put off—for the moment—the calling of a convention to consider secession. But Governor Strong was already mulling over the idea of a separate peace with England.

Though the New England Federalists could not know it, a peace process was beginning in January. Lord Castlereagh, who had rejected the Russian offer of mediation in the preceding year, said that he would negotiate directly with American representatives if they were sent to London. America demanded a neutral location, and Gothenburg in Sweden was chosen (soon transferred for convenience to Ghent in Belgium). On the peace commission Madison this time secured confirmation for Gallatin, since he included, as a concession to the "warhawks" in Congress, their spokesman Henry Clay. Gallatin, while trying to make peace with the British, had his hands full keeping peace between members of the peace commission, since Clay and John Quincy Adams "acted upon each other as explosives" (G 520).

Some in Congress feared that sending peace commissioners would weaken the war effort, making it impossible to hold out for favorable terms at Gothenburg. But keeping the war going would take far more men and money than Congress had supplied so far. George W. Campbell, who had taken over the Treasury Department from Gallatin, asked Congress to give him authority for borrowing twenty-nine million dollars devoted to the year's campaign, and he was given twenty-five (S 376). The banks best able to loan those sums, however, were in New England, and they were refusing to help the war effort. Campbell was forced to scrape together the amount from a number of smaller banks charging exorbitant interest. He wanted to restore the national bank, but Congress had not yet become desperate enough to reverse its ideological commitments on that issue. Madison, though, was persuaded in March to call off his embargo, since it was not so much hurting New England (which largely defied it) as the rest of the country.

THE PROFESSIONALS ARRIVE

What use to make of the men and money Congress was trying to supply was a subject on which Armstrong remained infuriatingly vague.
On the shores of Lake Ontario, he had replaced feuding generals
Wilkinson and Hampton with feuding generals Jacob Brown and
George Izard. But a new discipline in the regulars had been instituted
at the winter camps. This changed the complexion of the war. The
British, some of them veterans of service against Napoleon's troops,
had developed, by this point, a dismissive attitude toward the American fighting man. They had encountered mainly militia troops, drawn
from different states, with conflicting leadership, service terms, and
understanding of their duty. Their officers, with political bases in
their separate states, often refused to be led by the regular army.
Monroe would write to the Senate in the autumn of 1814:

> It may be stated with confidence that at least three times the
> force in militia has been employed at our principal cities,
> along the coast and on the frontier, in marching to and return-
> ing thence, than would have been necessary in regular troops;
> and that the expense attending it has been more than propor-
> tionately augmented from the difficulty, if not the impossibil-
> ity, of preserving the same degree of system in the militia as in
> the regular service. (A 1092)

The lack of discipline in the militia extended to the hygienic polic-
ing of their own camps, so that "five militiamen sickened and died
where one regular soldier suffered" (A 1062).

Winfield Scott thought the militia were "vermin"—militia had
watched as he was taken prisoner on Queenston Heights because
his fellow Americans would not cross the river to assist him.[1] During the winter 1813–14, Scott, who always traveled with his military library, established a training camp to drill the increasing
number of regulars, instilling a new discipline in them. At Plattsburgh, George Izard was doing the same thing. Izard, who had been
educated in European military schools, was the best drill instructor
in the American army, and when his five thousand regulars
marched to join the Scott-trained troops at Niagara, the war leaped

at once to a new level of professionalism. This was enhanced by the fact that the troops in the North could observe how the navy was working on the lakes. Midshipmen were not volunteers who could leave the ship the way militiamen fled a battlefield. Performing naval duties was a matter of survival for everyone on board. The blockading of the frigates on the coast had freed naval officers and men for service on Lakes Champlain, Ontario, and Erie. The first results of that had been seen in Perry's victory on Lake Erie. Veterans of frigate service were models for the land troops, as Perry had been for the troops he carried to the Battle of Thames River.

George Izard proved, like McClellan in the Civil War, better at training troops than at fighting them. His caution made Jacob Brown impatient. With Winfield Scott as his trusted subordinate, Brown cut through the vagueness of Armstrong, and the reluctance of Izard, to drive his troops toward a reconquest of Fort George. When he proved to have insufficient troops for that, the British tried to block his withdrawal at Chippewa on July 5, where Winfield Scott's brigade defeated a superior British force while taking heavy casualties.

> The battle of Chippewa was the only occasion during the war when equal bodies of regular troops met face to face, in extended lines on an open plain in broad daylight, without advantage of position; and never again after the combat was an army of American regulars beaten by British troops. Small as the affair was, and unimportant in military results, it gave to the United States army a character and pride it had never before possessed. (A 938)

After this victory, Brown returned to attack Fort George, but was again unable to mount an assault. He withdrew toward the Chippewa battlefield of three weeks earlier, stopping under Niagara Falls at Lundy's Lane, where there was another engagement with superior numbers. In a night battle of five hours, the Americans captured the British artillery and inflicted heavy casualties on the enemy, though at the cost of a third of their own numbers.

The respect the Americans had now instilled in the British forces was apparent when the wounded Brown ordered his subordinate,

Eleazor Ripley, to re-engage the enemy. Ripley took his depleted forces out to reconnoiter the British, exposing his men to the possibility of a crushing blow; but the enemy had now grown too cautious to deliver the blow. Ripley fell back to Fort Erie. The British were under orders to secure a large segment of American territory as a bargaining basis for the peace talks going on in Ghent. So a careful siege was laid upon Fort Erie; but it failed of its purpose on August 14. "For the fourth time in six weeks, a large body of British troops met a bloody and unparalleled check, if not rout, from an inferior force" (A 964). America had begun the war with the idea that Canada would be easy pickings. The British had ended the year 1813 with the symmetrical delusion that New York would be easy pickings. Brown and Scott dispelled that impression.

An even greater setback for the British was about to come, at the Battle of Plattsburgh on Lake Champlain, fought by water and land forces on September 11, two months after the bloody engagements at Niagara. The British navy had controlled Lake Champlain since the beginning of the war. But Thomas McDonough was preparing a small navy like that which Perry created on Lake Erie. McDonough was a veteran of war at Tripoli, where he served on the frigates *Constellation* and *Philadelphia*. He had been with Stephen Decatur in the daring raid that destroyed the *Philadelphia* after it fell into enemy hands. He was used to war, conventional and unconventional. His task at Plattsburgh was to prevent the British navy from giving artillery support to the British army as it was attacking the American fort there.

McDonough's own ship *Saratoga*, with twenty-six guns, was not a match on open water for the British *Confiance*, with thirty-seven guns. But he anchored his fourteen small vessels in the entry to the bay, where the sixteen British ships would have to fight their way past him to bring their guns within range of the Plattsburgh walls. The *Confiance* sailed up to the *Saratoga*, and they exchanged broadsides for over an hour, smashing the gun emplacements on the smaller ship. But McDonough had carefully prepared a little engineering marvel, based on two sets of anchors. Loosing one set, he used the other set to winch his ship completely around, unmasking the battery on the ship's uninjured side. The astonished British, who had thought McDonough beaten, had only four serviceable guns left on their own engaged (port) side, and they could not bring those to bear because *Confiance* was shipping water so fast that it had to shift the disabled port guns to the starboard side to stay afloat. Completely disarmed, the ship had to strike its colors after a two-hour struggle.[2]

The struggle was going so hard for the British in the North that a British fleet had been sent to create a diversion in the South. News of victory on Lake Champlain crisscrossed the country with news of loss coming from the Chesapeake Bay area. The capital had been seized and burnt.

11

Washington and Baltimore
(1814)

The burning of Washington (August 24, 1814) occurred a month after Brown vindicated the regular troops on the Canadian border, and a month before McDonough's victory at Lake Champlain. It was not as important, in military terms, as the other two events. In fact, it had little military effect at all. It was meant to strike a blow to American morale, and it did not even accomplish that. Anger and vengeance were activated more than despair, or even discouragement. Madison quickly brought the city back into operation. But the event is worth considering here—it amounts to a perfect study of what was wrong with Madison's conduct of the war. His intimate involvement with every aspect of this event is unlike his more remote connection with other developments; and his failure here explains much about setbacks elsewhere. There were four main causes of failure.

1. *Lack of intelligence.* Without some knowledge of the enemy's movements and intent, an army fights as Demosthenes said that a barbarian boxer does—holding each place on his body after it has been hit, never putting up a guard before the blow falls.[1] The American army had no regular system of scouts, no means of assessing and correlating reports of the enemy's activities. Reliance was placed on reading newspapers from England, Bermuda, Jamaica, etc. Or on the word of chance passersby. Or on the questioning of enemy prisoners

or deserters. In the case of the move on Washington, Armstrong, the secretary of war, debated with the general in charge of the area, William Winder, the numbers of British ships reported to be sailing for southern waters from Bermuda. Scouts had not been deployed on the Chesapeake to count the arriving ships.

After the fleet placed British troops ashore at the Chesapeake town of Benedict, a letter from the area was consulted, and two British deserters were asked by the president himself if the numbers landed were about the same as the numbers of American militia they saw around them. They said the numbers were about the same, though they were not—there were more militia (B 6.294–95). The lack of solid information meant that General Winder himself spent precious hours acting as a scout; and even Monroe, the secretary of state, rode as close as he dared to the enemy, trying to assess troop size. That two men of their rank were doing what was properly a subaltern's task shows how little thought had been given to intelligence gathering. The leader of the British troops, General Robert Ross, who had seen service against Napoleon's army in Spain, knew how to use his own scouts. He read accurately the lack of defensive moves against his five-day march along the Patuxent River. One of the officers with him said, "Jonathan is so confounded that he does not know when or where to look for us, and I do believe that he is at this moment so undecided and unprepared that it would require little force to burn Washington."[2]

The man was right. Without some solid basis for assessing enemy movements or intent, the Americans could not reach an agreement on the probable goal of the troops in their area. Armstrong thought they were going to Baltimore, or perhaps to Annapolis. Winder thought they would swerve west to attack shipyards on the Potomac, and he made a preliminary disposition of his force to meet this improbable move. Madison and Monroe thought that Washington was the target; but they did not countermand actions taken on the other two assumptions—which leads to the second flaw.

2. *Lack of a clear command structure.* In the early days of the war, Secretary of War Eustis had not defined the lines of responsibility between regular divisions. He had not overruled disputes about precedency, either in the regular army or between it and militia

officers. As a result, General Dearborn expressed repeated doubts about whether he had authority over Upper and Lower Canada (and thus over William Hull) or only over Lower Canada. Armstrong, when he took over the War Department, similarly failed to spell out the responsibilities of Wilkinson and Hampton. Nor had he and the secretary of the navy worked out the chain of command to link Isaac Chauncey's navy on Lake Ontario with action of the armies on its shore. So now, during the assault on Washington, Armstrong sometimes acted as if he were in charge but more often refused to intervene with Winder's arrangements, even when they seemed to him defective.

When the commander in chief himself, having ridden to the point where militia were being deployed at Bladensburg, asked Armstrong whether he had advised Winder on troop postings, Armstrong said no. The president suggested it was not too late for that, and Armstrong rode over toward Winder. Madison could not control his borrowed horse well enough to reach the two men as they conferred. But when he rejoined Armstrong and asked if he had changed the deployment, Armstrong said no, it was as good as could be expected (B 6.300). Rutland notes sardonically of this moment: "Whether he realized it or not, Armstrong's goose was cooked" (R 161–62). The disconnect between Armstrong and Winder was such that Monroe and Madison both felt they had to intervene directly, Monroe changing the disposition of the lines at Bladensburg and Madison ordering gunners to make a rapid deployment from the naval yards to Bladensburg. Armstrong felt that this just confirmed the suspicion he had entertained, from the outset, that Monroe was trying to take control away from him in the Washington area, an effort supported by the president when he chose Winder over the secretary of war's own candidate for command in Washington. Which brings us to the third flaw.

3. *The political basis for military appointments.* Since the dread of a "standing army" had deprived the United States of a professional corps of officers based on merit, one lasting through different political regimes, the president began with two main criteria for commissioning of officers. The first was Revolutionary experience, which was outdated and had proved disastrous in the war's first

year. The other was political connection—which seemed necessary as a way of ensuring loyalty from the state militias. The latter is what Madison relied on when he overrode Armstrong's attempt to put Moses Porter in charge of Washington's defense. Madison felt that a close relationship with the Maryland militia called for a Maryland appointee, and Winder had that qualification, if no other. He was the governor's brother. It was Madison's personal choice who earned this blistering description from Henry Adams:

> Neither William Hull, Alexander Smyth, Dearborn, Wilkinson, nor Winchester showed such incapacity as Winder either to organize, fortify, fight, or escape. When he might have prepared defenses, he acted as scout; when he might have fought, he still scouted; when he fought, he thought only of retreat; and whether scouting, retreating, or fighting, he never betrayed an idea. (A 1018)

But the root of the problem at Washington was not the hapless Winder, who might have performed adequately if given clear guidance. He was deprived of that because he had become a shuttlecock in the contest going on between Armstrong and Monroe.

Madison had followed political norms in appointing Armstrong, in an attempt to keep northern Republicans loyal to his administration. But Armstrong struck out on an independent path when he went north to supervise the troops. Madison rebuked Monroe for his suspicions about Armstrong's ambition; but Monroe was right— and Armstrong deserved dismissal for his attempt to use Wilkinson to advance his own devious plans. But Madison could not object to the use of Wilkinson, since he had kept him on because Jefferson protected him. Thus there were layers on layers of political considerations preventing the choice of competent military leaders.

Madison had expressed his displeasure to Armstrong for his tactics in the North, but he did not countermand the orders he thought mistaken (S 405). In the summer of 1814, while Madison was at Montpelier, Armstrong disobeyed the president's express order not to fill a vacancy caused by the retirement of General William Henry Harrison, when Armstrong made Andrew Jackson a major general on his own authority. Once again, Madison complained but did nothing further (S 399). Armstrong, instead of being chastened by these expressions of annoyance, just resented the president's vague way of interfering with his actions. Thus the federal city was exposed to the enemy because of political strife among those who should have been defending it—just as the northern armies had been subjected to the strife between Wilkinson and Hampton, Brown and Izard, Brown and Chauncey. Much of this political tension was based on the fourth flaw.

4. *Continued reliance on the militia.* Madison, remember, had felt that he had to appoint Winder to keep the loyalty of the Maryland militia, the troops within easiest reach from Washington. Yet when Winder tried to call up the militia for whatever the British were doing on the Patuxent, Armstrong said that the whole point of militia was their rapid summonability, and delayed the call. When the militia were activated, many arrived in haste and disorder, too late to be disposed wisely and made fully aware of their task. The result was that they bolted and ran at Bladensburg, six miles from the Capitol, even though they had a two-to-one advantage in numbers. Captain Mahan of the navy was no doubt influenced by his professional prejudices when he wrote:

> In the defenders of Bladensburg was realized Jefferson's ideal of a citizen soldiery, unskilled but strong in their love of home, flying to arms to oppose an invader; and they had every inspiring incentive to tenacity, for they and they only stood between the enemy and the center and heart of national life. The position they occupied, though unfortified, had many natural advantages, while the enemy had to cross a river which, while in part fordable, was nevertheless an obstacle to rapid action, especially when confronted by the superior artillery the Americans had.[3]

But Mahan is no harsher than a modern authority:

> With nearly six thousand militiamen and Barney's sailors, the Americans outnumbered the British, but many of the untried

militia riflemen were more eager to flee than to fight. . . . The vaunted militiamen had hightailed for home. Except for the moaning of the wounded and the distant rattle of the scattered, retreating army, all was quiet on the Blandensburg Road. It was only four o'clock; with plenty of daylight left, the British began to move down the pike toward Washington. Thus the victors, almost unopposed, made a leisurely march into the capital of the United States. A sniper killed [British commander] Ross's horse, after which a token force of three hundred armed Americans scattered. (R 162)

The president himself showed great courage during this whole sequence. He kept his head while others were growing hysterical. A week before the actual arrival of the British in Washington, rumors of their approach made nervous people gather outside the White House, suspicious that the Madisons would sneak off to save themselves (S 411). But Madison had no intention of fleeing. On August 22, he rode toward the enemy, staying overnight at Winder's camp near the naval yards. Back in Washington on the night of August 23, he rose early in the morning to move with Winder's camp to Bladensburg on the morning of the battle there. He personally took what turned out to be the most effective action of the day. Winder was going to leave Commodore Joshua Barney at the naval yards. Madison ordered the commodore and his four hundred navy artillery men to trundle their guns over toward Blandensburg.

Barney was the man in charge of a fleet of Jefferson's useless gunboats near the mouth of the Patuxent. When the boats were trapped upriver by Admiral Cockburn's fleet, Winder ordered Barney to leave them but to bring the guns off the boats to the naval yard. When Madison sent the guns on to Bladensburg, Barney arrived just as the British were passing through the town. Setting up his artillery in the path of the British army, Barney's men checked its advance while all other American forces fled. The sailors stuck to their guns until ammunition ran low and the British bayonets reached them. The enemy recognized these men's gallantry, in their dispatches home, and in their treatment of Barney:

"Barney himself, being wounded and unable to escape from loss of blood, was left a prisoner. Two of his officers were killed, and two wounded. The survivors stuck to him till he ordered them off the ground. [British General] Ross and [Admiral] Cockburn were brought to him, and greeted him with a marked respect."[4] While Barney was checking the enemy, Madison was at the White House, making sure his wife had got away:

> The President left Bladensburg battlefield toward two o'clock. He had already ridden in the early morning from the White House to the navy yard, and thence to Bladensburg—a distance of eight miles at the least. He had six miles to ride, on a very hot August day, over a road encumbered by fugitives. He was sixty-three years old, and had that day already been in the saddle since eight o'clock in the morning, probably without food. Soon after three o'clock he reached the White House, where all was confusion and flight. (A 1016)

Dolley had departed in her beloved and fashionable carriage (P 1.174), taking a few belongings with her, after rolling up Gilbert Stuart's full-length portrait of Washington and committing it to men who would keep it safe. At the State Department, important documents were being carried away (including the Declaration of Independence and the official diary of the Constitutional Convention).

General Ross camped the British troops at the city's edge, and at nightfall led a small contingent into the city to burn down the government offices. Private property was spared—though American looters took the opportunity for a little free-enterprise plundering (R 163). The very selectivity of the destruction would lead, in following weeks, to accusations that a traitor had guided the invaders to their proper targets. The restraint of Ross was rebuked when reports of it reached his own government, Lord Bathurst instructing him not to be so considerate in the future: "If, however, you should attack Baltimore, and could, consistent with that discipline which it is essential for you not to relax, make its inhabitant feel a little more the effects of your visit than what has been experienced at Washington, you would make the portion of the American people experience the consequences of the war who have most contributed to its continuance" (A 1128–29).

During the night of the fires in Washington, Madison and Dolley were unable to find each other—she stayed at one friend's home in Virginia, he in another. He met her the next day; then, assured of her safety, he went to consult with Winder, whose troops were on the road toward Baltimore. It was assumed, properly, that the fleet would move up to that city next. Madison, meanwhile, after almost four days and nights in the saddle, this frail little man on borrowed horses, went back to his numbed capital to re-establish the government. He turned the defense of the city over to Monroe, after learning that some troops had declared their determination not to obey Armstrong. Madison would not dismiss Armstrong on the spot, but he suggested he remove himself for a time. Armstrong left, and sent back a resignation from his first resting spot. With Winder in Baltimore, Monroe had become the acting general in Washington, as well as acting secretary of war. He began to fortify the city, uncertain whether other British troops would be arriving. Frigates did in fact approach Washington from the west, on the Potomac; but they were satisfied to take supplies and booty from the terrified town of Alexandria, which saved itself by capitulating. Madison wrote to Dolley suggesting she not return to Washington until he was sure the city was safe. But she was already on her way back to him.

It was suggested that Madison should summon Congress to a different, safer spot—Congress had, after all, been shifted about during the Revolution. But Madison knew the government must be seen to function, and he called Congress back for an early session. He had chambers prepared for the House and Senate in the Post Office and Patent Building, which had escaped the fires. He and Dolley moved into the house they had lived in when he was secretary of state—though the French minister, Louis Serurier, soon vacated his own residence, the current Octagon House, for their use. Dolley found those quarters too cramped, and she would end up in the former offices of the Treasury, where she could entertain on the scale she was used to. She, too, realized that it was important to return the city to its normal patterns. But the Madisons never returned to the blackened White House.

BALTIMORE

In Baltimore, though Madison had appointed Winder for his Maryland connections, Madison's old nemesis, Senator Samuel Smith, had no intention of turning over the defense of his city to a nincompoop. Using his own officer status in the militia as his credential, he took personal charge of the city's defense. Earthworks were thrown up on the land approach, and artillery posts were established at the entries to the harbor, manned by sailors under the command of navy officers. In effect, Smith had deployed effectively a whole swarm of Barneys. The guns of Fort McHenry were expertly directed by Lieutenant Colonel Armistead of the artillery. The sheet of fire thrown out from these installations kept the British ships at bay. Though the ships filled the night with "the rockets' red glare" celebrated by Francis Scott Key, Cockburn could not work them within range of the city, and all they achieved was illumination. Baltimore escaped capture by using the fortification skills that professionals had demonstrated elsewhere, and that Armstrong had declared unnecessary for the defense of Washington. One of the great advantages of the Americans in this war was the sophisticated engineering corps developed in the young academy at West Point. That corps did for the land war what America's naval architects did for war at sea.

Its chief was Colonel Joseph Gardner Swift, of Massachusetts, the first graduate of the academy. Colonel Swift planned the defenses of New York harbor. The lieutenant-colonel in 1812 was Walker Keith Armistead, of Virginia—the third graduate, who planned the defenses of Norfolk. Major William McRee, of North Carolina, became chief engineer to General Brown, and constructed the fortifications at Fort Erie, which cost the British General Gordon Drummond the loss of half his army, besides the mortification of defeat. Captain Eleazer Derby Wood, of New York, constructed Fort Meigs, which enabled Harrison to defeat the attack of Proctor in May, 1813. Captain Joseph Gilbert Totten, of New York, was chief engineer to General Izard at Plattsburgh, where he directed the fortification that stopped the advance of Prevost's great army. None of the works constructed by a graduate of West Point was captured by the enemy; and had an engineer been employed at Washington by Armstrong and Winder, the city would have been easily saved. (A 1341–42)

12

Maneuvering Out of War
(1814–1815)

Just before Washington was captured, Madison had met with a dispirited cabinet to go over early reports of what the British would be demanding at the Ghent peace conference. Gallatin had gone to London when the Russian mediation effort fell through, and he described for Madison the punitive atmosphere prevailing there. Far from meeting any of the five demands issued by Madison at the opening of hostilities, the English were calling for retaliation against America. To remove occasions for future conflict, a buffer zone of land should be annexed to Canada, sealing Americans off from the Great Lakes and the St. Lawrence River system. England's Indian allies in the struggle were to be rewarded with a great new nation carved out of the Northwest Territory. The popular mood in London was bitter. Madison was accused of helping Napoleon ("his Corsican master") when England was in mortal peril. He was the target of extraordinary personal vilification in the newspapers, ridiculed for his pompous treatises on sea law—"the lunatic ravings of the philosophic statesman of Washington," as the *Times* put it (A 1186). The paper even said that Louisiana, stolen from Spain with Napoleon's help while Madison was secretary of state, should be returned to Spain.

Madison at last recognized that he must give up on the matter of impressment, though Jefferson had urged him never to do that—impressment was, after all, the reason he (Jefferson) had turned down the treaty negotiated by Monroe in 1805. Just after Jefferson left the presidency, he warned his successor not to yield to Federalists ("a faction") wanting to strike a bargain with England:

It will confirm the English too in their practice of whipping us into a treaty. They did it in Jay's case, were near it in Monroe's and, on failure of that, have applied the scourge with tenfold vigor and now come on to try its effect. But it is the moment when we should prove our consistence by recurring to the principles we dictated to Monroe, the departure from which occasioned our rejection of his treaty, and by protesting against Jay's treaty being ever quoted, or looked at, or even mentioned. (P 1.139)

The grim terms expected hourly from Ghent convinced Madison that the days for such rodomontade were over. He was admitting, in effect, that his current secretary of state had been right in the struggle that caused their first dissension.

The American peace commission received the terms submitted by the British team of negotiators in October—and they amounted to a demand for capitulation. Almost all the Northwest Territory would be taken away from America and given to the Indians. Parts of New York and New England must be ceded to Canada. There was no concession to any of the American grievances cited as casus belli. The American delegates forwarded these demands to Washington, though they knew that Madison could not accept them and retain his office. They prepared to return to America, accepting the prospect of a war with no foreseeable end to it. But they did not appreciate the generous statesmanship of Lord Castlereagh, who had stopped by Ghent on his way to the larger diplomatic task of dismantling Napoleon's empire at the Congress of Vienna. Castlereagh did not like the way British negotiators were conducting themselves in Ghent, and he intervened to soften the terms. He realized that the British, despite their vexation with America, were also weary of two decades of war. Now that the life-or-death grapple with Napoleon was finally ended, keeping up hostilities with America would simply take a degree of psychic energy and financial sacrifice that would quickly become unpopular. He also realized that he would have a stronger hand to play at Vienna if he could assure the other powers that British attention would be concentrated, now, on Europe, without the distraction he called "the millstone of an American war."[1]

When the British signaled a change in approach, the task of statesmanship devolved on the American team, and it was Gallatin who made his fractious comrades live up to what was demanded of them. John Quincy Adams would not give up America's right to use Britain's Grand Banks fisheries, since his father had made that a key provision in the treaty that ended the Revolution. Henry Clay would not recognize the same treaty's guarantee of England's right to navigate the Mississippi, since that was a prerogative his western constituents were determined to monopolize. Gallatin wore down their insistence on explicit treatment of these rights. He saw that the one great issue had become territory. Was the treaty to recognize the holdings of the two powers at the cessation of hostility (*uti possidetis*) or go back to pre-war boundaries (*status quo ante bellum*)?

The British began with the *uti possidetis* principle, since they expected their army to have taken large chunks of land around the Great Lakes and around New Orleans by the time the treaty reached its ratification stage. But reports of the summer setbacks in the Niagara area and of the Battle of Plattsburgh, reaching Europe during the autumn of 1814, dashed those expectations. The British government turned to Napoleon's conqueror, Lord Wellington, asking him to take over command in America; but he read the recent reports and said that England could not make significant territorial gains in America except at costs the people were no longer willing to pay. He judged that failure to maintain naval control of the Great Lakes was the great failure of the war from England's point of view, and that a British general no more "possessed' American land than he could claim to own soil "over which his patrols pass." Sorting out priorities, Wellington concluded that if he went to Canada, it would be only "to sign a peace which might as well be signed now."[2]

After Wellington delivered this opinion in November, the *status quo ante* became the more realistic basis for negotiation. Among other things, the status quo would restore fishing rights to America and Mississippi navigation to England. Clay was persuaded to yield on the latter point so long as the matter was not expressly mentioned in the treaty. John Adams credited the success of the discussions to Gallatin's manipulative patience: "He has a faculty when discussion grows too warm of turning off its edge by a joke, which I envy him more than all his other talents; and he has in his character one of the most extraordinary combinations of stubbornness and of flexibility that I ever met with in man." That is not a bad definition of the diplomat. Nor is the sentence that followed, linking cleverness with deviousness: "His greatest fault I think to be an ingenuity sometimes trenching upon ingenuousness" (A 1219).

While this drama was playing out at the conference table in Belgium, fear of the terms England would impose had revived separatist talk in New England. A regional convention to consider secession, which had been proposed but not acted on in January, was revived in October. The Massachusetts legislature called for it to meet at Hartford. Madison feared the worst:

The greater part of the people in that quarter have been brought by their leaders, aided by their priests, under a delusion scarcely exceeded by that recorded in the period of witchcraft, and the leaders are becoming daily more desperate in the use they make of it. (K 193)

When the twenty-seven delegates met in the Connecticut State House on December 15, they went into secret session—an ominous thing, considering the precedent of the meeting at the Pennsylvania State House in 1787. Monroe moved troops to the Connecticut area, in case they were needed to put down an uprising as the convention disbanded (S 477). But when two New England states (New Hampshire and Vermont) refused to send a full delegation, Harrison Gray Otis, presiding at the convention, counseled moderation—it would be wise to see how the war went in the new year before taking their states out of the union. They should form a provisional union looking to another convention in Boston on June 15. After several weeks of suspense, the final recommendations were reported out on January 5. As a result, three commissioners (led by

Otis) were dispatched to Washington, where they would present a list of grievances, ask for several amendments to the Constitution, and demand a power to sequester federal taxes for use by the states in their own defense.

The proposed amendments to the Constitution descended to such pettiness as one aimed at Gallatin (denying any federal office to the foreign born) and another aimed at Monroe (prohibiting successive presidents from the same state). Madison laughed out loud when he read them—partly, no doubt, in relief that the volcanic mountain had produced such a mouse (R 186). But he could not be happy that the convention turned his own language of 1798 against him, propounding a state's authority "to interpose its authority for their [people's] protection." This, according to James Banner, "nationalized the doctrine of interposition."[3] The nationalizing process would come back to haunt Madison in his retirement, when secession took on a more threatening shape in his own region. Meanwhile, the change in the nature of New England thinking is described by Samuel Eliot Morison: "Thus for the third time within six years New England Federalism advanced Jeffersonian principles of state interposition, or nullification, in direct contradiction to the Federalism of Washington and Hamilton."[4] Party politics were being drastically rearranged by the war.

THE AFTERWAR

Though a peace treaty based on the *status quo ante* was being hammered out in Ghent in the final weeks of 1814, Madison could not know that yet. He had to prepare for another year of hard fighting, with more British troops freed from European service and streaming across the Atlantic. England's war strategy had not caught up with its peace initiative. The orders were still for His Majesty's forces to seize all the land possible, as the basis for new territorial arrangements in the final treaty. Early in the year, Madison had to consult with Brown on reinforcing the Niagara region and worry about an army of invasion dispatched to New Orleans under Wellington's own brother-in-law, Lord Pakenham. The fleet dispatched this time was larger than any yet sent across the Atlantic—sixty vessels, led by the eighty-gun ship of the line *Tonnant* ("Thunderer"). The massed force bore over a thousand cannon.[5] To meet this great peril, Madison and Monroe had to rely on the most successful general in the South, Andrew Jackson. He had proved that he could make even militia troops effective—but by his own peculiar methods. He did not rely simply on his charismatic energy and courage. When militiamen serving with him against the Creek Indians said that their enlistment time had elapsed and they were going home, he threatened to shoot anyone who did so, and he actually did execute one man (S 359–61). Madison was made uneasy by such high-handedness, and especially by Jackson's determination to capture East Florida at a time when Madison felt that could endanger international relations. Even when ordered to New Orleans in the summer of 1815, Jackson took time to seize Pensacola before heading west. (He gave as excuse the fact that the British might land at Pensacola in order to march several hundred miles to New Orleans.) His delay brought him to New Orleans almost too late. He arrived there on December 1, but left almost immediately to scout the situation along the Mississippi. By the time he returned, December 11, the British fleet was assembled at Cat Island, eighty miles from New Orleans. Jackson was absent again on December 15 when, in the evening, he heard that the British were entering the bayous.

He rushed back to the city the next morning and declared a state of emergency, imposing measures common in later wars, but ones that Congress and his own principles had denied to Madison—the imposition of martial law and curfew, suspension of habeas corpus, conscription, and censorship of the press. People on the street without passes could be arrested. Jackson had assumed dictatorial powers—in time he would arrest a judge who upheld a newspaper's right to criticize him. Jackson felt that the motley population of New Orleans made it hard to assess the loyalties of Spanish or French Creoles, freed blacks, organized pirates, friendly Choctaw Indians, and businessmen accustomed to trading with anyone who had ready cash. Jackson himself recruited Jean Lafitte's pirates only after the British had refused to meet the terms for their cooperation.

Jackson's energy differed pointedly from Winder's response in the attack on Washington. Jackson used engineers to throw up defenses, obstructing approaches to the city, entrenching artillery positions, using slave labor, free workmen, Creoles, and soldiers— any hands he could find. In the same way, he put together his army from all available materials, offending many when he put arms in the hands of freed blacks. He addressed the numerous blacks as "brave fellow citizens," and offered them the same bounty that was given white volunteers (160 acres of land).[6] He also used Choctaw Indians for swamp patrol and scouting.[7] The artillery men from the pirate ships were especially useful, not only for their practiced skill but for the abundant ammunition they commanded, their knowledge of the bayous, and the maps they supplied Jackson.

When British scouts found an approach that Jackson had not obstructed, by way of Lake Borgne, a party of the enemy came within seven miles of the city before Jackson was alerted to their presence on December 23. Informed at noon that they had set up camp, he did not wait for a possible attack from them in the morning, but hastily assembled a force of two thousand men to make a night raid on them. In the early darkness of December, he quietly moved up the American schooner *Carolina*, which had fourteen guns, now manned by the experienced pirates. At seven-thirty, when the *Carolina's* guns surprised the British at their campfires, Jackson led his men against troops silhouetted by the fire, making this the First Battle of New Orleans (December 23, the day before peace was concluded at Ghent). Jackson's men withdrew before midnight, having suffered twenty-four deaths and inflicted forty-six.

Jackson drew back two miles and began the feverish construction of earthworks. The Americans heard loud cheering from the enemy camp on Christmas day—Lord Pakenham had arrived with the main body of troops and the British artillery. On December 27, that artillery steadily chewed the *Carolina* to pieces. Jackson tried to flood the British camp by opening a levee, but the water did not rise high enough to help him. Instead, he moved the only other American schooner, the *Louisiana*, into a position where its guns could cover his embankment. When Pakenham sent seven thousand men against Jackson's four thousand at the earthworks, *Louisiana's* guns slashed through the lines of the assailants and the embankment's defenders did not give way (the Second Battle of New Orleans, December 28).

After the Second Battle, while Jackson was extending and strengthening his lines of defense, word came to him that the Louisiana legislature, convinced that the defense was doomed, was ready to surrender the city. In that case, Jackson said, somebody should "blow them up." The territorial governor, William Claiborne, who was frightened of Jackson, did indeed lock the legislature out of its chamber.[8] On the British side, Pakenham ordered heavier guns from the fleet to be wrestled through the bayous and put in place for an attack on New Year's morning. But Jackson's thickening artillery emplacements fought back successfully (the Third Battle of New Orleans, January 1, in which eleven Americans died, and twenty-six British).

On the day of the main engagement, January 8, British attempts at flanking Jackson's position through swamp and brakes failed, and the place where the central charge was made became a killing ground. British officers, trying to keep their men streaming across that ground, had to expose themselves to the cannon fire—Pakenham and two of his generals were killed. Only 13 Americans perished (largely freed blacks who scorned taking cover), while 192 British did. If all the casualties of the four engagements at New Orleans are added up—killed, missing, and wounded—there were 2,444 British to 336 American losses, "a ratio of about 7 to 1."[9]

Spectacular as the January victory in New Orleans was, it does not count as the last major engagement of the war, which continued at sea for several months. On January 15, Stephen Decatur's frigate *President* was engaged in unequal struggle with three British frigates, one of which he crippled before being forced to surrender. His frigate was later auctioned by the British in Bermuda. A happier fate awaited the *Constitution*, which ended the war as it had begun it, with a signal victory. Attacked on February 20 by two British sloops of war, *Cyane* and *Levant*, the *Constitution* outmaneuvered and outgunned them both, and was taking them as prizes back to America when it ran into a British squadron of three frigates on March 11. The *Constitution* and *Cyane* outran the squadron, but the *Levant* was peeled off by the pursuers. On March 23, the American sloop-of-war *Hornet* captured the British sloop *Penguin*, but had to leave it when chased by a British ship of the line. The *Constitution* brought *Cyane* home to a victory celebration three months after the peace terms were agreed on.

A VICTORY?

Washington was a gloomy place in January 1815. Draconian peace demands from England were still being discussed with a numb bitterness. New England was flirting with secession. No victories at sea had been reported for a long time. War was about to resume around Niagara. Worst of all, an apparently invincible fleet was besieging New Orleans. Then, in February, the city was so pummeled with good news that it became giddy with euphoria—some said with arrogance. Harrison Gray Otis, arriving with the demands made by the Hartford Convention, reached a town that could now afford to snub him: "We have received no invitation from Madison—what a mean and contemptible little blackguard" (K 597). The treaty was received with such relief that it was ratified by the Senate overnight (February 16). The news from New Orleans made Jackson an instant hero. Pride in the *Constitution* was renewed after its forced hibernation. The blockade was lifted. Prices of export goods soared. Prices of imports sank. There was a massive shudder of joy, as if great things had been achieved.

Logically, this feeling was hard to justify. The nation had struggled for two years and eight months to get back to where it started in the first place. Not a single one of its announced war goals had been reached. The entire basis of Republican commercial policy had been abandoned. The Americans in Ghent were not sure they would be returning to a grateful nation. Clay, in fact, expected obloquy. Adams said that they had cobbled out an armistice, not a real treaty, and one "hardly less difficult to preserve than [it was] to obtain."[10] But they had become heroes in their absence, and Madison rewarded them with important foreign ministries.

The negotiators who *were* treated with disrespect were the British spokesmen crossing from Ghent to London. Even those in England who wanted an end to the American war thought that their team had botched the conclusion. By publicly asking for so much at the outset and getting so little by the end, they created a sense that England was forced into peace rather than dispensing it from a superior position. The *Public Advertiser* called this a "degrading manner of terminating the war," and the *Times* hoped that Americans would reject the treaty and continue the war until Britain achieved a total conquest.

Then which side won the war? If we go by the vindication of the actions that brought on the war—the violations of neutrality at sea and impressment of American crews—then England did. Those practices were defended throughout and were still asserted at the end. Yet the practices had been vital to the British only because of the war with Napoleon. With that over, the need for them was drastically reduced, and they would decline in practice. If, on the other hand, Americans won the war, then what exactly did they win? And who or what did the winning? In one sense, Madison and the Republicans won. They resisted Federalist attacks on the war, and even on the union. They came out of the war with a sure hold on the presidency for at least another Virginian term, James Monroe's—which became, in fact, two successful terms. With one member of the old Federalist-Republican struggle reduced to fecklessness, a post-ideological "era of good feelings" dawned.

But did Republican *policies* win? If opposition to centralization, federal power, and nationalism was crucial to their policies, then John Randolph had a point when he said that they won by losing their souls. Jefferson had opposed the Bank of the United States, public debt, a navy, a standing army, American manufacturing, federally funded improvement of the interior, the role of a world power, military glory, an extensive foreign ministry, loose construction of the Constitution, and subordination of the states to the federal government. All those things were firmly back in place in the aftermath of the war. Madison's program for 1816 included a protective tariff for manufacturing interests, a permanent army staff, new ships for the navy, and internal improvements (though, in a gesture that was ignored, he asked to achieve the last item by constitutional amendment).

The nation had become enamored of military glory. The heroism, real or imagined, of military officers would fuel prominent careers for decades to come, for men like Oliver Hazard Perry, Stephen Decatur, and Winfield Scott. It would give real but less lasting fame to men like Isaac Hull (hero of *Constitution* battles), Jacob Brown (hero of Lundy's Lane), Joshua Barney (hero of Bladensburg), Thomas McDonough (hero of Plattsburgh). Five military veterans of the war would become president—James Monroe (secretary of war as well as commanding general of the Washington district), Andrew Jackson (hero of New Orleans), William Henry Harrison (supposed hero of Tippecanoe), John Tyler (captain of a Richmond brigade), and Zachary Taylor (hero of Fort Harrison). Not only did West Point win prestige and increased federal funds as a result of the war. Training camps of the sort Winfield Scott and George Izard had set up during the war were continued in peacetime. The nation was being readied psychologically for the use of power. Unlike Vietnam, which left the nation chary of future engagements, the War of 1812 left America itching for another fight.

13

—————

Assessing the Presidency
(1815–1817)

During his last year in office, Madison rode the swell of popular
nationalism. All parts of the government were operating smoothly,
after years of dysfunction. For the first time Madison had a competent and harmonious cabinet. His diplomatic team was highly qualified, stocked as it was with the veterans of the Ghent negotiation.
The Congress, obstructive during the war, became energetic and
efficient in peace. A whole generation of young men had come to
power and influence during the war. The Republican Party was
united for the first time in years. It could look forward to a smooth
succession in the 1816 election. For such a happy concatenation of
things a president is bound to get some credit.

How much of the credit did Madison deserve? After all, he
deliberately went to war with incompetent war secretaries and generals, with inadequate economic and military resources, with
reliance on an unfit militia. He accomplished not a single one of the
five goals he set for the war to achieve. In time, the incompetent
military leaders were weeded out, more by their own failures than
by Madison's guidance. "It took eighteen months for the dross of
the officer corps to settle at the bottom."[1] Given all these factors,
historians have not boosted Madison, considered as president, out
of the average rank. On the other hand, they do not count him a
failure—and they cannot. He was too popular at the end of his second term. He must have been doing something right. Despite all

the problems and setbacks of his chosen course, he never panicked. He was coolest at the darkest times. Admittedly, he was helped in this by his very flaws. In his provincialism and naivete he continued to underestimate the British, thinking they must have been badly harmed by his embargo.

Though members of his cabinet left in a storm of accusations against him—Robert Smith, William Eustis, Paul Hamilton, John Armstrong—he did not let himself get trapped in a cycle of recriminations. He wisely did not try to compel New England governors to cooperate with the war (except in his efforts against their trade). Despite what Andrew Jackson did in the truly desperate New Orleans situation, he did not himself violate the civil rights of a citizenry at war. His record on this is much better than that of Abraham Lincoln or Woodrow Wilson or Franklin Roosevelt. He did stretch the Constitution at times; but the most notable examples of this occurred before the war, not because of the war. He seized West Florida by presidential fiat. Joseph Story opposed—and Jefferson had misgivings about—his re-imposition of nonintercourse without congressional authorization. But during the war itself, as if to prove that the Constitution did not have to be jettisoned in a crisis, he was truer to its strictures than any subsequent war president.

War is a constant temptation to demagogy, and he never succumbed to it. Again he had the strength of his weaknesses. A man without the executive temperament inclines more slowly if at all to the dictatorial. Madison trusted the people to make adjustments that were being forced on them by circumstances beyond his control. It takes a certain wisdom to recognize just what is and what is not controllable. Because of his legislative temperament, he tried to help people put the pieces of the nation together in new patterns, instead of imposing a pattern of his own.

For a long time, Henry Adams set the terms of discussion for Madison's presidency—he wrote, after all, five superbly researched volumes on the subject. According to the most common (but simplistic) reading of those volumes, Madison was forced to abandon Republicanism and adopt Federalism in order to make the nation governable. But if Federalism prevailed, why did not the genuine spokesmen for that view inherit the outcome? Why did the nation still consider itself Republican, and vote for people it identified as such? Actually, what Madison was forced unconsciously to adopt was not an ideology but a historic phenomenon—modernity. The forces of modernization—technological, economic, secular, centralizing, populist—were associated partly with the British credit system and partly with the French military system.[2] But there was nothing unique to the Old World about these. In fact, Henry Adams was the first to identify the factors that made America particularly fitted for using new tools on ancient tasks.

The Federalists' mistake was to associate their favored forms of modernization—especially the credit system and centralized planning—with inherited class and religious concepts. The "Federalism" (so called) of Madison's America was, by contrast, meritocratic, technological, and secular. The new heroes were not conventional elites. They were people like the engineers from West Point. The skills employed on fortifications during the war would be used to build the Erie Canal in peace. The manufacturing complexes that built cannon during the war were soon turning out steamboats by the hundreds. The old class approach to military leadership was destroyed by the war. Social-leader generals were replaced by pragmatic populists like Andrew Jackson—John Quincy Adams was still living in the world of Federalist values when he denounced Harvard for giving an honorary degree to Jackson, a person who, Adams ungrammatically claimed, "could not write a sentence of grammar."[3] The old militias had been run by the political establishments of the states. The young officer corps of the regular army was now open to talent in the same way that the naval corps had been.

The clergy of New England were discredited when they opposed the War of 1812 as "godless." Madison reflected modern values when he refused to institute the customary day of prayer and fasting during time of war. When Congress asked him to issue a proclamation, he merely said people could pray if "so disposed" (P 4.581). He would not have done even that, he claimed, except that he could not afford a fight with Congress at that point. For the same reason, he did not try to abolish the chaplaincies of Congress and the military, though he thought them unconstitutional.[4] As it was, in telling people that they could pray if they wished, he returned to Washington's precedent, which was non-denominational, as opposed to the Christian terminology of John Adams's fast days.[5] Madison's neutral terminology brought many letters of protest. A self-identified "Bible Christian" was furious to find nothing in Madison's words that would "be offensive to the ear of a pagan, an infidel, a deist, and scarcely to that of an atheist" (B 6.199). The part of the Constitution that Madison was least likely to infringe was his favorite one, the separation of church and state. He exercised his veto three times to prevent state help to church buildings or supplies.[6] In the veto of February 21, 1811, he refused to incorporate a church in the District of Columbia because that would be "a precedent for giving to religious societies, as such, a legal agency" (P 3.176).

War is a centralizing force. Strategic planning, mobilization of resources across distances, more repaid communication, more ruthless promotion or demotion for competence—all these have to be adopted, by hard necessity. That can produce an authoritarian regime. Against any such tendency, Madison's scrupulous constitutionalism served the nation. Federalists thought that centralization involved concentrating all power in the hands of a few wise leaders, excluding others. The centralization that took place in 1812–15 was inclusive. It incorporated the energies and informality of the western territories. It made citizens more aware of the different parts of the nation. Psychologically, it shrank America. People huddled together. Tolerance grew. Dogmatism decreased. (These are all factors well analyzed by Adams in his concluding chapters on the Madison years.)

It makes little sense to ask whether Federalism or Republicanism won in 1815. Neither of them won. Nationalism did. The war eroded the purely ideological criterion for judging events. If we want to savor what the emotional impact was on intelligent observers at the time, we can turn to the opinions of people as different as the French minister Louis Serurier, or ex-president John Adams in his retirement, or Supreme Court justice Joseph Story.

Serurier, Napoleon's representative in Washington, had watched at close hand the whole process of beginning, waging, and concluding the war. He thought America was the clear winner because it had been boosted, in the process, to the position of a coming world power.

These three years of warfare have been a trial of the capacity of their institutions to sustain a state of war, a question . . . now resolved to their advantage. It has moreover had the good effect of destroying the illusions, the prejudice and the mental habits of too prolonged peace; of familiarizing the people with the carrying of arms, of reconciling them to the idea of taxes and the sacrifices necessary to their defense. . . . Finally, the war has given the Americans what they so essentially lacked, a national character founded on a glory common to all. . . . Glory has dissipated this prejudice [against a navy], and united all minds. You will notice that the President in his message has recommended progressive enlargement [of the navy]. . . . [The United States] are at this moment, in my eyes, a naval power. . . . Within ten years they will be masters in their waters and upon their coasts. (B 6.378)

America's navy victories on the sea, Serurier maintained, were "a prelude to the lofty destiny to which they are called on that element" (B 6.377).

Old John Adams took a rosier view of the war's outcome than did his son in Ghent. Writing to Thomas McKean in the summer of 1815, he said:

Mr. Madison's administration has proved great points, long disputed in Europe and America:

1. He has proved that an administration, under our present Constitution, can declare war.

2. That it can make peace.

3. That, money or no money, government or no government, Great Britain can never conquer this country or any considerable part of it.

4. That our officers and men by land are equal to any [of Wellington's forces] from Spain and Portugal.

5. That our navy is equal . . . to any that ever floated on the ocean.[7]

The man who saw most clearly the nationalistic implications of the war just concluded was Madison's first appointee to the

Supreme Court, Joseph Story. Though Story had denied Madison's right to resume nonintercourse without congressional authorization, he upheld many of Madison's war measures, and did so in the most hostile territory, the New England where he had to serve as circuit judge.[8] In the month when the treaty terms were received in Washington, he exulted in a great triumph:

Peace has come in a most welcome time to delight and astonish us. Never did a country occupy more lofty ground; we have stood the contest, single-handed, against the conqueror of Europe; and we are at peace, with all our blushing victories thick crowding on us. If I do not much mistake, we shall attain to a very high character abroad, as well as crush domestic faction. Never was there a more glorious opportunity for the Republican party to place themselves permanently in power. They have now a golden opportunity; I pray God that it may not be thrown away. Let us extend the national authority over the whole extent of power given by the Constitution. Let us have great military and naval schools; an adequate regular army; the broad foundations laid of a permanent navy; a national bank; a national system of bankruptcy; a great navigation act; a general survey of our ports, and appointments of port-wardens and pilots; judicial courts which shall embrace the whole constitutional powers; national notaries; public and national justices of the peace, of the commercial and national concerns of the United States. By such enlarged and liberal institutions, the government of the United States will be endeared to the people, and the factions of the great states will be rendered harmless. Let us prevent the possibility of a division by creating great national interests which shall bind us in an indissoluble chain.[9]

Story's paragraph sounds like Jefferson's worst nightmare, here masquerading as a Republican victory. If the Federalists were anachronistic in their defense of modernizing tools, Republicans were anachronistic in adopting those tools without shedding the rhetoric of bucolic local amateurism, the language of gentlemen managers of large estates who liked to pose as "farmers." Jefferson thought that Story had gone over to John Marshall's Federalism once he was on the court. But Story's biographer, R. Kent Newmyer, argues persuasively that the Republican Story's nationalism was his own from the outset—he anticipated or outran much of Marshall's centralizing adjudication, most notably by a case decided in the war's afterglow (on March 20, 1816), *Martin v. Hunter's Lessee.* This case, in which Virginia's courts had for years denied federal jurisdiction over land rights contested since the Revolution, "was a landmark in the history of federal judicial supremacy. More even than Marshall, Story upheld federal judicial supremacy over the states."[10] Story wrote:

> The Constitution of the United States was ordained and established not by the states in their sovereign capacities but emphatically, as the preamble of the Constitution declared, by "the people of the United States.". . . It is a mistake that the Constitution was not designed to operate upon states in their corporate capacity. It is crowded with provisions which restrain or annul the sovereignty of the states in some of the highest branches of their prerogative . . . the states are stripped of some of the highest attributes of sovereignty, and the same are given to the United States. (A 1312)

These words no doubt expressed Story's abiding conviction; but his biographer is no doubt right in saying that they would not have been expressed so pungently, or received so passively, but for the nationalist fervor created by the war. So Madison was carried by events toward a modernity he neither anticipated nor desired. But he was able to ride the Constitution he had fashioned, steering it through the tumultuous transition, and bring it to a new place essentially unharmed.

Epilogue:
The Legacy

When Madison left office in 1817, he was sixty-six years old, but Dolley was only forty-nine, and she wanted to visit Paris, from which she had been ordering her gowns for years. He said they could not afford it; his plantation was shrinking as he was forced to sell off land and slaves. She would return to live in Washington after his death; but for the next twelve years they did not leave the neighborhood of Montpelier. In 1829, however, he took her with him to Richmond, since he was a delegate to the convention for revising Virginia's constitution. It was his fourth constitutional convention. He was the only delegate there who had attended the first two (Virginia's state convention of 1776 and the Philadelphia convention of 1787), but his old disciple and later foe, John Marshall, was present from Virginia's constitutional ratifying convention of 1788—they had become allies again on things like internal improvements.

Madison, the master committeeman, was back in harness at age seventy-eight, diligently attending in the front seats during three months of acrimonious debate, acting as chairman of the legislation committee, trying to forge the last great compromises of his legislative career. The overriding issue of the convention was reapportionment. In Virginia, the districts were apportioned by population, including slaves. Since owners in the eastern region of the state had more slaves, western districts felt (and were) underrepresented in the legislature, outvoted by the patriarchs of Tidewater. The west wanted to count population on a "white-basis" only, and Madison began as a spokesman for his region—though he tried to split the difference by leaving the old mode of counting in the Senate and introducing white-basis in the House. When this satisfied neither side, he reverted to his own older compromise, dating from the Continental Congress and enshrined in the Constitution, counting slaves in the population at a three-fifths rate ("the federal number"). The eastern interests defeated this, and the dominant theme of Madison's later years, slavery, was all too clearly driving events. The great legislator could not get the convention to accept compromise. The patriarchs won. Slavery won. Madison was dismayed, though he tried to put the best face he could on the outcome. As Drew McCoy writes in a sensitive study of Madison's last years: "The convention of 1829, we might say, pushed Madison steadily toward the brink of self-delusion, if not despair. The dilemma of slavery undid him."[1]

The slavery issue was forced on the aging Madison because its defenders now invoked his and Jefferson's secessionist language of 1798. Madison hid as long as he could the fact that Jefferson was the author of the Kentucky Resolutions, and that the original draft of those Resolutions contained nullifying language. He had embarrassingly denied that any such thing was ever considered.[2] He also tried to fudge or downplay his own terminology of "interposition," though John C. Calhoun logically argued that if one authority is "placed between" the citizen and another authority, the latter one is estopped.[3] As Madison went obsessively over his old papers, he tried to impose an artificial consistency on them, or to tidy them up with regard to later views—antedating, for instance, his hostility to Hamilton, or muting criticisms of men like Washington and Lafayette, or fuzzing over the shifts in his approach to states' sovereignty.

Julian Boyd, the editor of Jefferson's papers, caught him in an egregious falsification. To eliminate criticism of Lafayette in a coded letter he wrote to Jefferson, he not only deleted original passages but faked Jefferson's handwriting to alter the recipient's decipherment of his letter (J 7.451). The backroom reconciler of other people's disagreements in committee tried to harmonize himself with himself. To downplay his role in the Virginia Resolutions, he got Jefferson to remove his defense of them from the curriculum of the University of Virginia (RL 1925). He even wanted *The Federalist* removed too, since John Taylor of Caroline had made that book part of the dispute over secession (RL 1924). Madison had always opposed the publication, during his own lifetime, of the proceedings of the Constitutional Convention—not only his own notes, but the official record. He knew the value of his notes, and wanted them to bring money to his estate for Dolley's use as his plantation failed—he was hoping for one hundred thousand dollars from sale of his papers, of which the notes were the gem (K 664). But in finally opening up this treasure, he tried to place it in a context that would take the edges off the inevitable reversals and contradictions of a life spent trying to accommodate principle to political reality. It was his very strength as a legislative reconciler that was at war with any abstract unalterability.

He felt little need to alter the record of his presidency, though the "Detached Memoranda" exaggerate somewhat his opposition to tax exemption for churches—he vetoed one example of that, but let two others of equal significance (which he does not mention) pass into law.[4] His greatest concern was for what he called the misuse of his doctrine of interposition to defend southern secessionism. Irving Brant noticed how worried Madison was about appearing inconsistent when his own secretary of the Treasury asked for a renewal of the Bank of the United States and the president was afraid to express his support publicly. When the nullifiers called him inconsistent on state sovereignty, the gravity of the matter was added to his concern for his own record. Others have plausibly argued that his guilt over complicity with slavery, which lay at the root of the nullification arguments about tariff, caused much of his disturbance. McCoy writes:

During the final six years of his life, amid a sea of personal [financial] troubles that threatened to engulf him, Madison could not get the nullifiers out of his mind. At times mental agitation issued in physical collapse. For the better part of a year in 1831 and 1832 he was bedridden, if not silenced, by a joint attack of severe rheumatism and chronic bilious fever. Literally sick with anxiety, he began to despair of his ability to make himself understood by his fellow citizens.[5]

Some admirers of Madison have taken his retrospective correc-
tions of the record at face value, arguing for a consistency throughout his life. There is no need for such cosmetic concern. No one
admired Madison more than Brant did; yet he never denied that the
man contradicted himself. The essential greatness is not canceled by
that fact—probably no great politician's could be. Madison's claim
on our admiration does not rest on a perfect consistency, any more
than it rests on his presidency. He has other virtues, which I want to
emphasize once more in this conclusion. In discussing his presidency, I had to leave out larger achievements. Among this nation's
founders, only two were more important—Washington and Franklin
(the *sine quibus non*). As a framer and defender of the Constitution
he had no peer—James Wilson came in second, but by a long distance. The finest part of Madison's performance as president was
his concern for preserving the Constitution. As a champion of religious liberty he is equal, perhaps superior, to Jefferson—and no one
else is in the running. Even if he is to be considered merely as a
writer, only Jefferson and Franklin were manifestly greater stylists.
No man could do everything for the country—not even Washington. Madison did more than most, and did some things better than
any. That is quite enough.

Notes

INTRODUCTION: THE PROBLEM

1. He hovers around number twelve in the listings. See the charts in Robert K. Murray and Tim H. Blessing, *Greatness in the White House: Rating the Presidents*, second edition (Pennsylvania State University Press, 1994), pp. 16–17.
2. Admirers or defenders add inches to short men—some claiming that Madison was five feet six inches—though the same height is given to his wife, and people found that she was noticeably taller than he, indeed that "Mrs. Madison dwarfed her husband." Conover Hunt-Jones, *Dolley and the "Great Little Madison"* (American Institute of Architects Foundation, 1977), p. 13.
3. Harold G. Syrett and Jacob E. Cook, editors, *The Papers of Alexander Hamilton* (Columbia University Press, 1961), 5.488.
4. Is it only coincidence that the three early secretaries of state who did have foreign experience performed well? They were Jefferson under Washington, Marshall as Adams's second secretary, and Monroe as Madison's second secretary.
5. Hunt-Jones, op. cit., p. 12.

1: BEFORE THE CONSTITUTION (1751–1785)

1. The war's ordeal made the South draw on its property in humans. In order to raise recruits for the Continental army, Virginia offered anyone who would sign up for three years the bounty of a slave, in good health, between ten and thirty years of age (2.185). Madison thought it would be easier to put slaves directly into the army, with a promise of freedom after three years. He said this would not undermine the

institution of slavery, since "a freedman immediately loses all attachment and sympathy with his former fellow slaves" (2.209).

2: THE CONSTITUTION (1786–1788)

1. W. W. Abbot et al., editors, *The Papers of George Washington*, Confed-
   erate Series 5 (University of Virginia, 1997), pp. 79–80.
2. Douglass Adair, *Fame and the Founding Fathers*, edited by Trevor Col-
   bourn (Norton, 1974), p. 134.
3. Cf. Charles F. Hobson, "The Negative on State Laws: James Madison,
   the Constitution, and the Crisis of Republican Government," *William
   and Mary Quarterly* 36 (1979), pp. 215–35.
4. William M. Bowsky, *A Medieval Italian Commune: Siena Under the
   Nine, 1287–1355* (University of California Press, 1981), pp. 109–10:
   "The prestige, ambition, family connections, and in some cases wealth of
   these [native Sienese] men impelled the oligarchy to keep them out of
   Sienese courts and to staff those courts with foreigners, whose lack of
   local family connections, brief residence in the city, and dependence
   upon the commune for income would keep them relatively honest. . . ."
5. Merrill Jensen et al., editors, *The Documentary History of the Ratification of the Constitution* (State Historical Society of Wisconsin, 1976–),
   vol. 10, p. 417.

3: THREE ADMINISTRATIONS (1789–1809)

1. Lance Banning, *The Sacred Fire of Liberty* (Cornell University Press,
   1995), p. 271.
2. Stuart Leiberger, *Founding Friendship: George Washington, James
   Madison, and the Creation of the American Republic* (University of
   Virginia, 1999), p. 207.
3. Ibid., p. 209.
4. Ibid., p. 137
5. Stanley Elkins and Eric McKitrick, *The Age of Federalism* (Oxford
   University Press, 1993), p. 263.
6. Ibid., p. 360.
7. Eugene R. Sheridan, "Thomas Jefferson and the Giles Resolutions,"
   William and Mary Quarterly 49 (1992), pp. 589–608.
8. Leiberger, op. cit., p. 215.
9. Noble E. Cunningham, Jr., *The Process of Government Under Jefferson*
   (Princeton University Press, 1978), pp. 283–87.
10. Merrill D. Peterson, editor, *Thomas Jefferson: Writings* (Library of
    America, 1980), p. 454.
11. Ibid., p. 1050.
12. Andrew A. Lipscomb and Albert Bergh, *The Writings of Thomas
    Jefferson* (Thomas Jefferson Memorial Association, 1903–4), vol. 12,
    pp. 375–76.
13. Leonard Levy, *Jefferson and Civil Liberties: The Darker Side* (Harvard
    University Press, 1963), pp. 119, 137.

14. Lipscombe and Bergh, op. cit., p. 194.
15. Ibid., p.160.

4: POLICY AND PERSONNEL (1809)

1. Henry Adams, *History of the United States of America During the Administrations of Thomas Jefferson* (Library of America, 1986), pp. 1172, 1245–46.
2. Leonard D. White, *The Jeffersonians* (Free Press, 1951), p. 7.
3. Dumas Malone, *Jefferson the President, Second Term* (Little, Brown and Company, 1974), pp. 622–26.
4. Robert M. Johnstone, Jr., *Jefferson and the Presidency: Leadership in the Young Republic* (Cornell University Press, 1978), p. 287.
5. Richard Mannix argues that Jefferson's withdrawal into himself actually began in the fall of 1807, a year before the time when most people recognized it, and was manifested in his oddly disengaged attitude toward the embargo, the details of which he kept turning over to Gallatin: Richard Mannix, "Gallatin, Jefferson, and the Embargo of 1808," *Diplomatic History* 3 (1979), pp. 151–72.
6. Stuart Leibiger, *Founding Friendship* (University of Virginia, 1999), p.178.
7. James Madison, *Letters and Other Writings*, vol. 4, pp. 491–92.
8. Irving Brant, Madison's loyal biographer, tries to downplay the importance of the Wilkinson decision, trivializing Wilkinson as a "black sheep of the army" and not giving the details of his offense (B 177, 352).

5: DOMESTIC AFFAIRS: THE PARTISANS (1809–1816)

1. Forrest McDonald, *The Presidency of Thomas Jefferson* (University Press of Kansas, 1976), p. 47.
2. James Madison, *Writings*, edited by Jack N. Rakove (Library of America, 1999), p. 714.
3. Robert W. Patrick, *Florida Fiasco* (University of Georgia Press, 1954), p. 10.
4. In the list of reasons given for this occupation, Madison actually included a claim that he was preventing the slave trade into America.
5. Patrick, op. cit., pp. 281–82.

6: FOREIGN AFFAIRS: SUCKERED TWICE (1809–1810)

1. C. S. Forester, *The Naval War of 1812* (Michael Joseph, Ltd., 1957), pp. 15–18, 34.
2. R. Kent Newmyer, *Supreme Court Justice Joseph Story* (University of North Carolina Press, 1985), p. 87 (the *Orono* case).

7: MANEUVERING INTO WAR (1811–1812)

1. Helen A. Cooper et al., *John Trumbull: The Hand and Spirit of a Painter* (Yale, 1982), p. 75.

9: FRIGATES AND A FRESH START (1812)

1. Marshall Smelser, *The Congress Founds the Navy, 1787–1798* (University of Notre Dame Press, 1959), p. 203.
2. Jonathan Elliot, *Debates of the Several State Conventions* (J. B. Lippincott Company, 1836), vol. 3, p. 309.
3. Smelser, op. cit., pp. 79–80.
4. C. S. Forester, *The Naval War of 1812* (Michael Joseph, Ltd., 1957), p. 38.
5. Ibid., pp. 24–25.
6. Ibid., pp. 41–42.
7. Theodore Roosevelt, *The Naval War of 1812* (Modern Library, 1999), p. 19.

10: PEACE OVERTURES AND PROFESSIONALISM (1813–1814)

1. Timothy D. Johnson, *Winfield Scott: The Quest for Military Glory* (University Press of Kansas), p. 26.
2. Alfred Thayer Mahan, *Sea Power in Its Relations to the War of 1812* (Little, Brown, and Company, 1905), vol. 2, p. 380.

11: WASHINGTON AND BALTIMORE (1814)

1. Demosthenes, *First Oration Against Philip*, 51.
2. Donald R. Hickey, *The War of 1812: A Forgotten Conflict* (University of Illinois Press, 1990), p. 197.
3. Alfred Thayer Mahan, *Sea Power in Its Relations to the War of 1812* (Little, Brown, and Company, 1905), vol. 2, pp. 349–50.
4. Ibid., p. 348.

12: MANEUVERING OUT OF WAR (1814–1815)

1. Bradford Perkins, *Castlereagh and Adams: England and the United States, 1812–1832* (University of California Press, 1964), p. 152.
2. Ibid., p. 109.
3. James M. Banner, Jr., *To the Hartford Convention: The Federalists and the Origins of Party Politics in Massachusetts, 1789–1815* (Knopf, 1970), p. 349.
4. Samuel Eliot Morison, *Harrison Gray Otis* (Houghton Mifflin, 1913), vol. 2, pp. 105–6.
5. Robert V. Remini, *The Battle of New Orleans* (Viking, 1999), p. 40.
6. Ibid., p. 38.

7. Wilburt S. Brown, *The Amphibious Campaign for West Florida and Louisiana, 1814–1815* (University of Alabama Press, 1969), pp. 109, 113, 179.
8. Ibid., pp. 118–19.
9. John W. Mahon, *The War of 1812* (Da Capo Press, 1972), p. 368.
10. Perkins, op. cit., p. 130.

13: ASSESSING THE PRESIDENCY (1815–1817)

1. Timothy D. Johnson, *Winfield Scott: The Quest for Military Glory* (University Press of Kansas, 1998), p. 22.
2. The British credit system is a recognized factor in Madison's final year as president. The French military influence is less familiar. But both the principal organizers of military discipline, Winfield Scott and Thomas Izard, were students of the latest French military theory, especially that of Baron Jomini. See Johnson, op. cit., pp. 50, 274 n. 25.
3. Robert V. Remini, *Andrew Jackson* (Johns Hopkins University Press, 1984), vol. 3, p. 78.
4. James Madison, "Detached Memoranda," *Writings*, edited by Jack N. Rakove (Library of America, 1999), pp. 762–64.
5. Ibid., p. 765.
6. Ibid., p. 760. For the vetos see Leo Pfeiffer, "Madison's 'Detached Memoranda': Then and Now," in Merrill D. Peterson and Robert C. Vaughan, editors, *The Virginia Statutes for Religious Freedom* (Cambridge University Press, 1988), pp. 288–95.
7. Bradford Perkins, *Castlereagh and Adams: Europe and the United States, 1812–1832* (University of California Press, 1964), p. 150.
8. R. Kent Newmyer, *Supreme Court Justice Joseph Story* (University of North Carolina Press, 1985), pp. 83–92.
9. William W. Story, *Life and Letters of Joseph Story* (Little and Brown, 1851), vol. 1, p. 254.
10. Kermit L. Hall, "*Martin v. Hunter's Lessee*," in Kermit L. Hall et al., *The Oxford Companion to the Supreme Court of the United States* (Oxford, 1992), p. 529.

EPILOGUE: THE LEGACY

1. Drew R. McCoy, *The Last of the Fathers: James Madison and the Republican Legacy* (Cambridge University Press, 1989), p. 252.
2. *The Writings of James Madison*, edited by Gaillard Hunt (Putnam, 1900–1910), vol. 9, pp. 402–3.
3. John C. Calhoun, "The Fort Hill Address" (1831), in Ross M. Lence, editor, *Union and Liberty: The Political Philosophy of John C. Calhoun* (Liberty Fund, 1992), p. 371. Madison actually used "interposition" for a military occupation in 1811 (P 3.93).
4. Leo Pfeiffer, "Madison's 'Detached Memoranda': Then and Now," in Merrill D. Peterson and Robert C. Vaughan, editors, *The Virginia Statutes for Religious Freedom* (Cambridge University Press, 1988), pp. 293–95.
5. McCoy, op. cit., p. 151.

Milestones

1751 Born in Virginia.
1769–71 Studies at Princeton.
1776 Delegate to Virginia Convention.
1777–78 Member of Virginia Council of State.
1780–83 Delegate to Continental Congress.
1785 Member Virginia House of Delegates, promotes Religious Freedom Act.
1786 Attends Annapolis Convention.
1787 Delegate to Constitutional Convention, leading drafter of Constitution.
1788 Delegate to Continental Congress, writes twenty-nine *Federalist* Numbers.
       Delegate to Virginia ratifying convention, defends Constitution.
1789–97 Member of House of Representatives.
1789 Drafts amendments to Constitution (Bill of Rights).
1795 Opposes Jay Treaty.
1798 Drafts Virginia Resolutions against Alien and Sedition Laws.
1800 Publishes *Report* defending Virginia Resolutions.
1801–9 Secretary of state.
1801 Louisiana Purchase.
1806 Publishes *An Examination* condemning British maritime practices.

1809–17 President of the United States.

1809 Erskine affairs (mistakes British message, restores trade).

1810 Cadore letter (mistakes French message, bans British trade).
Occupies West Florida.

1811 Secretly authorized to obtain East Florida.
William Henry Harrison battles Shawnees at Tippecanoe.
Bank of United States charter lapses.

1812 Declares war on England.
Detroit surrendered to British; invasion of Canada fails.
First naval victories.

1813 Tsar Alexander tries to negotiate end of war.
Oliver Hazard Perry's naval victory on Lake Erie.

1814 Battles of Chippewa and Lundy's Lane.
Capitol and White House burned down by British; Baltimore withstands attacks.
Naval victory at Plattsburgh.
Andrew Jackson defeats Creek Indians at Horseshoe Bend.
Hartford Convention discusses disunion.
Peace talks held at Ghent.

1815 Peace treaty ratified.
Andrew Jackson wins Battle of New Orleans.

1816 Second Bank of the United States chartered.

1817–36 In retirement at Virginia plantation (Montpelier).

1829 Delegate to Virginia Constitutional Convention.

1836 Dies at Montpelier.

Selected Bibliography

Madison's papers are being published in three series

The Papers of James Madison, edited by William T. Hutchinson et al.
(University Presses of Chicago and Virginia, 1962–)
The Papers of James Madison, Secretary of State Series, edited by Robert J.
Brugger et al. (University Press of Virginia, 1986–)
The Papers of James Madison, Presidential Series, edited by Robert A. Rut-
land et al. (University Press of Virginia, 1984–)

Biographies

Irving Brant, James Madison, volumes 1–6 (Bobbs-Merrill Co.,
1941–1961). The most thorough life, full of useful information.
Ralph Ketcham, James Madison: A Biography (University Press of
Virginia, 1971). The best one-volume life.

The Presidency

Henry Adams, History of the United States of America During the Administrations of James Madison, volumes 1–5 (Charles Scribner's Sons,
1889–91), printed as a single volume in The Library of America
(1986). The classic study, long standard.
Robert Rutland, The Presidency of James Madison (University Press of
Kansas, 1990). Excellent account by an editor of the Madison
papers.

The War of 1812

J. C. A. Stagg, *Mr. Madison's War: Politics, Diplomacy and Warfare in the Early American Republic, 1783–1830* (Princeton University Press, 1983). The best account of the war's political and economic, as well as military, aspects, by another editor of Madison's papers.

C. S. Forester, *The Naval War of 1812* (Michael Joseph, Ltd., 1957). Exciting account of the sea battles.

Index

ABOUT THE AUTHOR

Garry Wills, an adjunct professor of history at Northwestern University, won the Pulitzer Prize and the
National Book Critics Circle Award for *Lincoln at Gettysburg*. He is the author of *Saint Augustine* and *Papal Sin*.